08-04-2020

To Deb —

With hope for all people
in our world —

Peace,

David Walbly

Retreating Forward

Retreating Forward

A Spiritual Practice with Transgender Persons

DAVID ELIAS WEEKLEY

Foreword by David Equality Watters

RESOURCE *Publications* · Eugene, Oregon

RETREATING FORWARD
A Spiritual Practice with Transgender Persons

Resource Publications
An Imprint of Wipf and Stock Publishers
199 W. 8th Ave., Suite 3
Eugene, OR 97401

www.wipfandstock.com

PAPERBACK ISBN: 978-1-5326-0553-6
HARDCOVER ISBN: 978-1-5326-0555-0
EBOOK ISBN: 978-1-5326-0554-3

Manufactured in the U.S.A.   MARCH 6, 2017

With much love and respect, I dedicate this work to
Bishop Calvin D. and Velma Duell-McConnell,
two of my chosen family whose love and support made it possible.

Contents

Foreword

BY DAVID EQUALITY WATTERS

In "*Retreating Forward: A Spiritual Practice with Transgender Persons,*" David Weekley writes in a persuasive, intelligent and logical style. His key point, regarding how a retreat ministry might begin to undo the detrimental effects of adverse religious experiences among transgender persons, is clearly stated and explored thoroughly. Weekley coherently presents his research into this timely subject with insight and focus. His writing is accessible and relevant to a broad range of readers, both academics and non-academics alike.

We live in an era where spiritual awareness is becoming increasingly significant and many are seeking answers to questions about life's purpose and meaning, many are looking beyond the constraints of their physical, mortal limits to seek a greater, more profound understanding of their existence and many face damaging cognitive dissonance when attempting to reconcile faith and gender identity, when faced with disapproval and exclusion from traditional religious organizations. External sources of rejection can lead to internalized rejection of oneself and when that attack is upon ones right to explore and express ones spiritual nature, the damage can be immense.

Weekley brings a fresh perspective on how transgender and gender non-conforming individuals can access their spiritual path in a supportive and welcoming context. His writing is vital and life-affirming because it offers hope to those who need it most and it has the power to rationally enlighten those who may benefit from a broader understanding of the basic human desire (and right) to enjoy a spiritual life.

David Equality Watters is a National Diversity Award winner, teacher, motivational speaker, writer; and passionate equality advocate committed to enhancing the lives of young people and adults who may feel marginalized or limited by labels. "The Give 'em Hope" campaign was honored at the national diversity awards 2014 when it won the community organization award (multi-strand).

Watters was also a key player in the equal love campaign UK, which took the British government to the European court of human rights in 2010; which played a significant part in successfully securing marriage equality for same-sex couples in the United Kingdom.

Preface

This text explores how a retreat ministry grounded in the type of radical hospitality described by Jesus in The Parable of the Good Samaritan may begin to amend the harmful effects of negative religious experiences among transgender persons. As many faith communities seek meaningful ways to offer practical ministry with and for transgender persons this book provides one practice as a step in an ongoing process of education, community building, and practical theology. As the reader will discover through feedback from retreatants who participated in the retreat described within these pages, this proved to be a supportive practice and tool for engaging in ministry with transgender and gender non-conforming people seeking spiritual companionship.

Acknowledgments

With deep gratitude and loving respect, I thank five people whose guidance, encouragement, and support provided hope and inspiration along this journey: Dr. Mary Elizabeth Moore, Dean of Boston University School of Theology; Dr. Claire Wolfteich, Associate Professor of Practical Theology and Primary Advisor; Bishop Susan Hassinger, Bishop in Residence and Lecturer in Spirituality; and my beloved spouse, Deborah. A special thanks to Peterson Thomas Toscano whose friendship, creativity and comic relief added depth and joy to this work.

I am also thankful to the colleagues and peers who took the time to read, review, and comment on this text. Professor Phyllis Asnien, teacher of Humanities and life-long friend; Dr. Pamela Lightsey, Associate Dean and Clinical Assistant Professor at Boston University School of Theology, and author of *"Our Lives Matter: A Womanist Queer Theology;* Dr. Virginia Mollenkott, Professor and author of the Lamda Literary Award-winning, *Omnigender: A Transreligious Approach;* The Rev. Dr. Erin Swenson, Psychotherapist and Human Resource Consultant; The Rev. Dr. Justin Tanis, Managing Director, Center for LGBTQ and Gender Studies in Religion at Pacific School of Religion, and the author of, *Transgendered: Ministry, Theology, and Communities of Faith;* and Dr. Clare Watkins, Lecturer Ministerial Theology at University of Roehampton in London and co-author of, *"Talking about God in Practice."*

List of Abbreviations

lgbtq   lesbian, gay, bisexual, transgender and queer-identified

PAR   Participatory Action Research

TAR   Theological Action Research

Glossary

Cis-gender: Those whose gender matches the biological sex assigned to them at birth.

Gender non-conforming: Refers to persons who do not follow conventional ideas or stereotypes about gender roles; for example, how one should act or look based on the sex assigned at birth.

Gender-Queer: Persons who do not subscribe to conventional gender distinctions or roles but identify with neither, both, or a combination of male and female genders.

Intersex: The medical term and sometimes the self-identifying term for those born with indeterminate or mixed genitalia. These infants were often assigned a gender at birth based upon what appeared most appropriate to the medical team, although this practice is less common now.

Transgender: Persons who self-identify as a gender other than the one assigned at birth. This includes but is not limited to those who have medically transitioned.

1

Invitation to Hospitality

Transgender and gender non-conforming persons often suffer spiritual alienation, isolation, and desolation. Many in this community express a sense of alienation from institutional religion and a struggle to find spiritual community. Indeed, they face discrimination at every turn.[1] Events such as the dramatic rise in hate crimes following recent elections in the United States underscore the need for a supportive, responsive ministry on the part of faith communities who seek to stand in solidarity with transgender persons. The following pages are an invitation into a conversation about the theological foundations and existing need for such a practice. The text presents some historical background and resource literature, and describes Christian-based hospitality through the example of a spiritual retreat model for and with transgender and gender non-conforming persons. The retreat that evolved through theological reflection, conversation, and research is based upon participatory action research, a methodology that worked well within my theological framework of seeking to give voice to marginalized populations.

Theologian Elizabeth Conde-Frazier describes participatory action research as one way to accompany others in their suffering and struggles and to work together in responding to challenges and issues in their lives and community.[2] While this text does not focus on this methodology, it is important to note it was the operating method engaged when building the retreat with participants. Conde-Frazier describes it as incarnational research, involving people in formulating solutions for their problems, set-

1. Grant et al., "Injustice at Every Turn."
2. Conde-Frazier, "Participatory Action Research," 241.

ting agendas, reflecting theologically, and acting.[3] In this text, transgender and gender non-conforming people are engaged in reflecting on their lives, identifying their problems and concerns, setting goals, reflecting theologically, and developing strategies for future action. In a time when transgender persons are experiencing increased push-back from some religious organizations as well as segments of secular society, this type of process and experience may be significant for both the retreatants and those who facilitate it, including faith communities that develop and support such a ministry.

The theological grounding of this work is Jesus' "Parable of the Good Samaritan," found in the gospel of Luke 10:25–37. The Christian life is one committed to following the example and teaching of Jesus, drawing upon discernment and the Spirit for direction in life. Regardless of theological differences or preferred translation of sacred Scriptures, one essential mandate preceding all others is love of God and neighbor. This directive is found in several places in both the Hebrew Scriptures and the gospel, but the story told by Jesus in this parable powerfully underscores this directive. Above all else, this is a story of radical love and hospitality that precedes religious tradition or dogma:

> Just then a lawyer stood up to test Jesus. "Teacher," he said, "what must I do to inherit eternal life?" He said to him, "What is written in the law? What do you read there?" He answered, "You shall love the Lord your God with all your heart, and with all your soul, and with all your strength, and with all your mind; and your neighbor as yourself." And he said to him, "You have given the right answer; do this, and you will live."
>
> But wanting to justify himself, he asked Jesus, "And who is my neighbor?" Jesus replied, "A man was going down from Jerusalem to Jericho, and fell into the hands of robbers, who stripped him, beat him, and went away, leaving him half dead. Now by chance a priest was going down that road; and when he saw him, he passed by on the other side. So likewise, a Levite, when he came to the place and saw him, passed by on the other side. But a Samaritan while traveling came near him; and when he saw him, he was moved with pity. He went to him and bandaged his wounds, having poured oil and wine on them. Then he put him on his own animal, brought him to an inn, and took care of him. The next day he took out two denarii, gave them to the innkeeper, and said, 'Take care of him; and when I come back, I will repay you

3. Ibid., 246

whatever more you spend.' Which of these three, do you think, was a neighbor to the man who fell into the hands of the robbers?" He said, "The one who showed him mercy." Jesus said to him, "Go and do likewise."

This core story and teaching of Jesus relates directly to the invitation made in this text, and it was operative from the beginning as I envisioned a spiritual place of healing for both a population that often feels beaten, robbed, and abandoned by society; and faith communities isolated from their transgender siblings in faith as the result of unfamiliarity, fear, lack of information, or restricted theological education.

Like Samaritans and the dead in the time of Jesus, transgender and gender non-conforming persons today are one of the most marginalized populations on earth. This has been illustrated repeatedly by surveys such as, "Injustice at Every Turn" and the rising numbers of deaths reported each year during Transgender Day of Remembrance observances.[4] Despite such a clear example in the teaching of Jesus concerning right relationship between God and neighbor, many denominations and local congregations continue to either ignore or vilify the existence of this entire community. They are like those in Jesus' parable who, driven by fear of contamination and social rejection themselves, evade contact with the wounded victim, even crossing the road to avoid being proximate to one viewed as unclean. Such behaviors are not limited to individuals or even faith communities. Promises to "roll back" legal protections for transgender persons is among one of the campaign promises of the newly elected Trump administration. Proposals to allow discrimination against transgender persons by physicians, hospitals, and businesses are already under consideration through what is known as, "The Religious Freedom Act."

It is important to clarify that transgender persons do not always fall into the role of victim. The parable invites cis-gender and transgender persons to explore how they represent one role or another at various points over a lifetime. For example, at the age of fifteen when I first told an adult my story and transgender experience I felt very much like a victim. I felt fearful and vulnerable. Some of this was from the bullying and stigma I had already experienced in social life, especially school. Some of this was simply part of being an adolescent. Over time and with intentional acts of healing I moved from this perspective.

---

4. Grant, et al, "The National Transgender Discrimination Survey."

Like others, I have sometimes been among those who see someone in need but, due to lack of courage, a sense of mistrust, frustration that I can do so little, or something else entirely, instead of stopping to assist I "pass by" as it were, "on the other side of the road." In hindsight, these are not my best moments or memories, even when I understand that the personal risk involved appeared overwhelming at the time.

Whether transgender or cis-gender, becoming the Good Samaritan Jesus describes involves a lifetime commitment to a set of values that includes recognizing the innate worth and interconnectedness of every person. These values command the response to act and practice these values in life. The parable reveals the responsibility and potential contained in loving God and neighbor, as new relationships are formed between persons who, in a different paradigm, would be enemies. In Jesus' story the pattern changes, as the fallen victim and the Samaritan are *both* disdained, though for different reasons; one because he was believed to be ritually unclean, and the other because of cultural and religious practices. Like others, at my best moments I have embraced the stranger, offered hospitality, and broadened the circle of human relationships. On rarer occasions, I have filled a role like the innkeeper, providing a safe space, basic needs, and whatever healing I may offer to another traveling life's road.[5] Transgender persons, no less than cis-gender, are more than one-dimensional; and while it is true that too often transgender persons are victims, we are also resilient and just as likely to fit the other characters in Jesus' story.

Jesus describes authentic human relationship through the roles depicted in this parable. This provides an image and model for faith-based hospitality and the creation of authentic community today. The social and spiritual wounds of transgender and gender non-conforming people are addressed by collaborative and participatory ministries that foster spiritual companionship and renewal. I say this following decades of experience in parish ministry, specialized coursework in spirituality studies, and personal experience as a transgender man. Therefore, the text focuses on spiritual renewal and spiritual companionship ministry with transgender and gender non-conforming persons. Such ministry moves beyond abstract theological debate to acts of solidarity with a highly-marginalized population; the exact subject of Jesus' Parable of the Good Samaritan.

I come to this work after more than three decades of ordained ministry in the United Methodist Church, including the last nine years as an

---

5. Thank-you to Justin Tanis for comments around these various roles and images.

"out" transgender United Methodist clergy in Portland, Oregon, currently serving a pastorate in Hull, Massachusetts. These experiences led to meetings and conversations with literally hundreds of transgender and gender non-conforming persons of faith that continue to expand and unfold. One common element that stands out for many is the experience of rejection from their faith community when they risked coming out as transgender, and an ensuing isolation from spiritual companionship and community.

While there are positive stories of acceptance and celebration when transgender persons share their stories in their faith community, these are not the majority. Many people shared, and continue to share, stories of rejection, subsequent spiritual crises, and counter-rejection. Such narratives inspired me to reflect on Jesus' teaching about hospitality in The Parable of the Good Samaritan. What might such hospitality look like today among a faith community and a group of transgender and gender non-conforming persons? While the retreat I designed and facilitated certainly does not produce large-scale empirical data regarding transgender spirituality, it does involve close reading of Jesus' parable and deep listening to the spiritual autobiographies and questions of a small group of transgender persons in such a way that informs the development of a practical ministry grounded in hospitality for these same persons. A retreat like this may play a significant part in similar ministries.

An overnight retreat became important for me because so many transgender persons with whom I spoke expressed few or no opportunities to gather in a safe space for relaxed conversation, personal reflection, and spiritual renewal. Some told me they had never been to any kind of event with other transgender or gender non-conforming people. With these things in mind I began to reflect on the meaning of spiritual hospitality for such a diverse, scattered, and often isolated community.

The history of Christian hospitality as a spiritual practice goes back to at least the fourth century C.E. After Christianity became the state religion under Constantine, many women and men seeking an ascetic and spiritually centered life left their towns and communities to establish makeshift homes/cells in isolated places, especially in the Scetes desert of Egypt. Those who entered this life became known as an *abba* or *amma*, someone known to be wise and spiritually developed. Sometimes these wise people became spiritual directors for others, instructing them not primarily by formal theological instruction, but through the means of story, example, paradox, and spiritual encouragement. Although their living conditions were sparse and resources few, these early spiritual teachers offered a radical form of hospitality to other seekers, particularly beginners. The basic pattern of hospitality included a safe space to rest, food and beverage, and spiritual companionship. This model of hospitality continued to expand and develop over the centuries taking many forms and springing from several traditions; but these basic elements and practices of radical hospitality remained central to every form and style of Spiritual Direction. The retreat was designed to be a similar space of hospitality. The theme of the retreat was "Narrative and Spiritual Autobiography as Sources of Spiritual Renewal" and was grounded in spiritual hospitality and companionship as defined by authors like Margaret Guenther: "The spiritual director is a host who gives to her guests, the bestower of guest-friendship. She is a host in the truest and deepest sense, reflecting the abundant hospitality shown by the host at the heavenly banquet."[6] Marjorie J. Thompson also provided an excellent discussion on spiritual direction and spiritual companionship in *Soul Feast: An Invitation to the Christian Spiritual Life*.[7] Closely connected to hospitality is the practice of what Margaret Guenther terms "Holy Listening"—bringing one's full presence and attention to the practice of listening to narrative.[8] This is a practice both modeled and discussed during the retreat.

Amy G. Oden is one author who speaks of the connection between the gospel, hospitality, and spiritual companioning as a new way of seeing and living in the world:

> Gospel hospitality is God's welcome, a welcome that is deep and wide. Gospel hospitality is God's welcome into a new way of seeing and living. Ultimately, gospel hospitality is God's welcome into abundant life . . . Gospel hospitality almost always entails some kind of risk and leaves all parties changed. As we participate in gospel hospitality, God's welcome becomes a way of life that we share with the world.[9]

In the retreat described within this book, we explored this concept and practice of hospitality, both as co-creators of and participants in this kind of hospitality.

---

6. Guenther, *Holy Listening*, 10.

7. Thompson, *Soul Feast*, 107–24.

8. Ibid., 1.

9. Oden, *God's Welcome*, 11.

The retreat also emphasized creative expression through the arts. In addition to hospitality and spiritual companionship, self-expression through art is another practice through which persons may experience Divine hospitality and companionship. Drawing upon connections made between spiritual direction and the arts through authors such as Christine Valters-Paintner and Betsey Beckman, the retreat engaged and encouraged self-expression by participants through written, visual, auditory and other forms of art.[10]

Hospitality, spiritual companionship, and creative expression create a positive atmosphere in which to explore reading, writing, and sharing spiritual autobiography. The intention here is to develop a connection between spiritual companioning and spiritual autobiography, especially reflecting on the potential of spiritual autobiography to give expression to marginalized voices.[11]

One tool of participatory action research I employed in working with others in creating our retreat together was the use of interviews and questionnaires. The information gained through these tools helped inform and design a retreat-based spiritual ministry with transgender and gender non-conforming persons. This book does not claim to produce replicable data but rather to unfold a method of spiritual companioning in a particular context; to reflect on the process of designing that ministry so as to critically inform and inspire such collaborative envisioning in the future; and to encourage spiritual ministries with transgender persons in other contexts. The text incorporates interviews with fourteen transgender persons who were participants in the retreat. In keeping with methods of participatory action research, I understood each participant to be a co-creator of our time together. Attending to the particularities of their spiritual questions, hungers, and practices facilitated how to build and design the theme, and the time we spent together.

The book describes an overnight retreat focused on the abovementioned theme of "Narrative and Spiritual Autobiography as Sources of Spiritual Renewal." Reflection on the practice of designing and facilitating this retreat was continually focused on The Parable of the Good Samaritan, and the theme of hospitality.

10. Valters-Paintner, and Beckman, *Awakening the Creative Spirit.* See Part 1 for a discussion of spiritual direction and the arts.

11. Phan and Young Lee, eds., *Journeys at the Margins.* This resource provides reflection and examples of spiritual autobiography from the perspective of marginalization and "other."

Participatory action research worked well as my method because of its participatory structure and reflective process, eliminating the sense of subject-object asymmetry and replacing it with subject-subject symmetry.[12] In other words, the playing field is levelled; everyone participates equally. While often practiced in educational settings and other human-serving organizations, this method is especially useful in developing a retreat for transgender and gender non-conforming people. In adopting action research as my method I followed Elaine Graham, a prominent scholar in the field of practical theology, who asserts that practical theology itself can be understood as a form of action research.[13]

Historically, participatory action research is based on three components: (1): popular education, defined as self-education by the group or organization for the purpose of social change; (2): action research, which includes collaboration with community organizations to improve life quality; and (3): participatory research, which involves participants of the group or organization in the research process and in creating better models for future development.[14] I applied these same principles to the design of my retreat intended for spiritual renewal and companionship ministry with transgender participants.

In *Talking About God In Practice: Theological Action Research and Practical Theology*, authors Helen Cameron, Deborah Bhatti, Catherine Duce, James Sweeney, and Clare Watkins apply action research to practical theology.[15] They identify this form of action research as theological action research. Their approach provided a good method for exploring hospitality because it is collaborative; is immersed in theology and theological conversation at every point; recognizes various influences on personal and communal theology; follows conversational method; and seeks to transform practice, incorporating previous practice and experience into the process.[16] Such a process resonated with the isolation often voiced in the stories told to me by other transgender persons of faith. Following the retreat, I conducted another round of interviews with my co-creators with the following aims: assessment of the overall experience of the retreat both in structure

12. Miller-McLemore, "The Emergence of Participatory Action Research," 7419, Kindle.

13. Graham, "Is Practical Theology a Form of 'Action Research'?" 148–78.

14. Strand, et al, *Community-Based Research and Higher Education*, 4.

15. Cameron, et al, *Talking About God In Practice*.

16. Cameron, et al, 51–59.

and content; conversation and analysis of each component of the retreat based upon participant feedback; evaluating whether the retreat began to ameliorate spiritual isolation; and building upon this experience to plan future retreats.

As this book illustrates, providing hospitality, a safe and welcoming space in which transgender and gender-queer persons can explore spiritual autobiography, narrative, and practices may begin a healing process. Such a space may reveal important dimensions of transgender spirituality and of- fer faith-communities a model for proactive ministry with the transgender community.

2

Who is My Neighbor?

The lawyer in Jesus' parable wants to limit those who fall within the definition of neighbor. In response Jesus tells a story that removes all boundaries of the classification, offering an extreme example of inclusivity. Some people today, even those who follow Jesus attempt to draw similar boundaries. There are those who attempt to place transgender and gender non-conforming persons outside the circle of neighbor through legal actions, political activism, and religious dogmatism. Despite such endeavors the parable stands as a basic truth per Jesus: there is no one outside the definition of neighbor. Transgender and gender non-conforming persons are your neighbors. The goal of this chapter is to describe this population for those who are unfamiliar or know little about us.

A key to understanding the suffering, spiritual pain, and religious alienation of those who identify as transgender and gender non-conforming is knowledge of past and current social history. Exploring this landscape helps begin a theological conversation about the need for new and proactive spiritual ministries with and for transgender persons. Transgender people exist in virtually every culture, so providing an extensive historical overview is beyond the scope of this book. The beginning of this chapter will provide a brief overview of various attitudes towards transgender persons, but will focus on the example of European behavior that began with Native Americans, sometimes known as "Two-Spirit" people after Europeans arrived in North American. I chose this focus because Western European culture, including political, religious, economic and other social systems are the bedrock of prevailing tensions concerning social attitudes and policies directed towards transgender and gender non-conforming people.

The next part of this chapter moves toward contemporary attitudes and examples. This section includes recent statistics, and a few examples taken from recent news to help readers comprehend the immensity of this problem of continued misunderstanding, lack of education, and policies and practices of oppression. The cost is immeasurable in terms of human life lost. It is important to say at this point that transgender people are robust. Despite social and religious pressure and persecution many succeed in living happy and satisfying lives. Overall, however, transgender and gender non-conforming people face discrimination and daily pressures not understood by the public. Therefore, it is important to examine some of the historical and current attitudes which adversely affect transgender people today. As the following pages illustrate the resultant effects of discrimination are many, including the increased risk of suicide, isolation, poverty, homelessness, and criminal violence. Percentages for any of these conditions increases for transgender and gender non-conforming persons of color. Acts of open discrimination and violence have significantly increased since the 2016 presidential election in the United States. Some perpetrators say they believe it is now socially acceptable to give voice and action to their transphobia.

One story in this chapter originates from my own ministry experience and is the personal story of a transgender woman seeking a welcoming and hospitable spiritual community. The chapter concludes with an exploration of possible practices a congregation may embrace to offer genuine hospitality and welcome to transgender persons.

Transgender persons exist in every culture known in recorded and current human history.[1] In some cultures and eras transgender persons are regarded as spiritually gifted persons, serving as spiritual leaders, shamans, counselors and valued members of the community.[2] While not formally educated as an historian, the late Leslie Feinberg spent years compiling a now classic text on transgender history as experienced by a member of this community. Feinberg noted, "Two-Spirit" or gender-fluid people were recognized, accepted, and often esteemed in virtually every Native American culture.[3] When European colonization began conquering these cultures,

---

1. Feinberg, *Transgender Warriors,* Parts 2 and 3 of this text are particularly helpful in understanding the diverse responses to transgender persons throughout recorded history and into present 21st century American culture.

2. Ibid., 28.

3. Ibid., 21–22.

this included the imposition of a rigid, gender-binary deeply ensconced within their religio-political system. Under this oppression Two-Spirit persons were vilified and brutalized. From these conquering Europeans Two-Spirit persons received the derogatory term, "Berdache." A Berdache was any person who appeared androgynous. A 1594 engraving by Theodor de Bry depicts Balboa employing the use of dogs to kill Native American Two-Spirit persons while Balboa and other spectators casually observed.[4] History past and present, secular and sacred contains myriad examples of such mixed reactions and responses to transgender individuals.

Within Church history, the story of Joan of Arc is one of the most well-known and well-documented stories of transphobia within medieval Christianity. Believing herself led by God Joan of Arc emerged as a leader during the Hundred Year War. The French were desperate to drive the English army from France and place Prince Charles on the throne. Dressed in male clothing Joan and a group of followers traveled to the court of Prince Charles, where Joan declared she was directed by God with a mission to drive out the English. She also declared that God mandated her male attire. Charles placed the seventeen-year-old at the head of a 10,000-member peasant army.

Following a successful march on Orleans, Prince Charles was crowned King of France with Joan standing beside him. On May 23, 1430, Joan was captured by the Burgundians, French allies of the English. The Burgundians referred to Joan of Arc as "homasse"-a slur meaning "man-woman."[5] Unlike a traditional knight, Joan was not ransomed back by King Charles but was handed over to the Catholic church for trial and condemnation because of her cross-dressing and masculine behavior.[6] Joan of Arc was executed and burned alive on May 30, 1431, in Rouen. She was nineteen years old.[7] To the end, Joan insisted God directed her to dress as a man, wear her hair cut as a man, and engage in traditionally male-gendered activities. From this history to current diverse and harmful policies directed toward transgender individuals, the Church has been a powerful prosecutor and oppressor of transgender and gender non-conforming people.

The much-publicized transition of Christine Jorgenson in the 1950's brought the term "transsexual" to public attention for the first time in

4. Feinberg, *Transgender Warriors*, 29.

5. Ibid., 32–33.

6. Feinberg, *Transgender Warriors*, 35.

7. Ibid., 36.

twentieth century American culture, although she was not the first person to undergo surgery or live a gender at variance with the one assigned at birth. There were others long before her, but most lived with their gender identity hidden. Jazz great and band leader Billy Tipton is one well-known example of a transgender person who lived "stealth" (secretly) most of his life. Born Dorothy Lucille Tipton, Dorothy became "Billy" as an adolescent and, following a brief period of presenting as male only in performance, quickly shifted into life as a man. Billy Tipton was so secretive that even his adopted sons did not know of his biological sex until the time of his death at age seventy-four.[8]

Beginning in the 1930s, transgender persons were undergoing sex reassignment surgery with the support of Magnus Hirschfield, a well-known German sexologist.[9] But Christine Jorgenson became a public sensation when her story was leaked to the press by an angry friend and she returned home to the United States to find herself greeted by three hundred members of the press. This much-publicized event threw Jorgenson under a social spotlight of sexual sensationalism from which she could not escape. Speaking of this in her autobiography Jorgenson remarked:

> At one time or another, I had been called a male homosexual, a female homosexual, a Transvestite, an hermaphrodite, a woman since birth who had devised a sensational method of notoriety for financial gain, a true male masquerading as a female, or a totally sexless creature-the last category placing me in the same neutral corner as a table or chair.
>
> Another surprising fact was brought to my attention during this critical survey, one that hadn't occurred to me before. Never once, in all those acres of newsprint had I been asked about my faith and beliefs, both of which had played important roles in my life. What I slept in, apparently, was considered more important.[10]

Christine Jorgensen expressed what many transgender people experience when their gender identity becomes public; a sexualization of the person. Unlike cultures such as the Navajo and Apache, United States culture followed early colonists such as Balboa in viewing transgender persons as overly sexual, perverse, and evil; a threat to Church, society, state and home that needed to be suppressed, strictly controlled, and eradicated. Despite

---

8. Middlebrook, *Suits Me: The Double Life of Billy Tipton*, 6

9. Jorgensen, *Christine Jorgensen: A Personal Autobiography*, vii.

10. Ibid., xvii.

such persecution over the centuries, transgender persons continued to seek legal protections, positive ways to live authentically, to be fully recognized as valuable members of the community, and to seek spiritual community.

The nineteen-sixties brought the birth of "Gender Identity Clinics" to the United States. The first clinic was established at John Hopkins University in 1966. On November 21 that same year the *New York Times* published a lengthy article attempting to explain male-to-female transgender persons (the only publicly known examples of that time), and the medical and psychiatric reasons for performing what was then known as "sex-reassignment-surgery."[11] These clinics operated under the strict guidelines of the Harry Benjamin Foundation which outlined a precise path and set of procedures for both male-to-female, and female-to-male transgender persons. The guidelines strongly encouraged post-surgical individuals to create an entirely new life and even a false history, not sharing one's transgender identity unless absolutely necessary.

This was the message I heard as I moved through the process of medical transition in Cleveland, Ohio in the nineteen seventies. I was told it was safer and would be easier for my future life than sharing my authentic history. I was encouraged to move away from the area in which I grew up, and to prepare to lose a few friends. Having now experienced life from both sides of life, first living "stealth" and today very openly as transgender, I experience some differences. Life is easier and safer as "just one of the boys/girls" if you pass easily (i.e. look like others of your gender based upon cultural cues) at least until something happens. A medical emergency, a social service need, a background check for employment, seeking a mortgage, or renting an apartment can immediately reveal personal history. Many circumstances can reveal personal information, and when that happens in the midst of an uneducated, or ill-educated culture transgender people are often the victims of oppression, discrimination, and violent crime.

Along with the rise of Gender Identity clinics came the appearance of an initial social acceptance of transgender persons. Presented as an unalterable mental condition, the most common recommended treatment for those identified as transgender was a complete physical transition through sex-reassignment surgery. Initially this solution gained acceptance and several Gender Identity clinics were formed around the United States. But push-back, vilification and objectification of transgender people began almost immediately. The two groups most vocal in objecting to transition

11. Jorgensen, *Christine Jorgensen*, 303.

related surgery were self-identified trans-exclusionary radical feminists[12] and some segments of the Christian Church. For example, Janice Raymond, a known feminist and gender essentialist, wrote much of the legislation presented during the Reagan administration that led to the abolishment of health insurance for transgender related health care. In one report, she wrote of the controversial nature of transgender identity:

> Over and above the medical and scientific issues, it would also appear that transsexual surgery is controversial in our society. For example, Thomas Szasz has asked whether an old person who desires to be young suffers from the "disease" of being a "tran-schronological" or does the poor person who wants to be rich suffer from the "disease" of being a "transeconomical?" (Szasz 1979). Some have held that it would be preferable to modify society's sex role expectations of men and women than to modify either the body or the mind of individuals to fit those expectations.[13]

Statements such as this and others related to transgender persons helped justify the exclusion of gender related health care from insurance policies, contributed to the perception of transgender persons as delusional, and conflated gender identity with current societal sex role expectations. Ecclesial objections to transition-related surgery contributed to such attitudes as well.[14]

A growing unwillingness to remain silent on the part of transgender persons has led to increased public debate and mixed response in terms of social support and positive public policy. For example, there are increasing numbers of Federal laws protecting the rights of transgender persons in terms of employment, health care, housing, and other areas of life. In 2012 the Equal Employment Opportunity Commission ruled that gender identity is included under gender in federal laws; a significant step. Following years of opposition, the U.S. Senate passed an inclusive Employment Non-Discrimination Act in 2014 that would have banned employment discrimination in the United States based upon sexual orientation or gender identity; however, the bill was not approved by the United States House

12. Trans-exclusionary radical feminism (or TERF) is a subgroup of feminism characterized by transphobia. Not a term endorsed by such feminists, they accept only the gender one is assigned at birth as legitimate and support gender essentialism.

13. Williams, "Fact Checking Janice Raymond: The NCHCT Report," *The Transadvocate*.

14. Norton, "Vatican Says 'Sex-Change' Operation Does Not Change Person's Gender," *Catholic News Service*, http://ncronline.org/news/vatican-says-sex-change-operation-does-not-change-persons-gender

of Representatives and failed to become law. Many states and cities have passed protections. The state of California passed the first state law giving K-12 students access to the use of school facilities of the appropriate gender, and to participate in the correct sex-segregated sports and other activities that correspond to expressed gender identity.[15] At the same time, some states and cities have passed more restrictive laws, or they employ other measures to marginalize, devalue, and disempower transgender persons. The state of Michigan provided one example of how quickly advocates of civil rights abandon transgender persons when Republican Frank Foster removed the inclusion of transgender persons from a non-discrimination bill in hiring and housing when pressed by constituents.[16] On March 24, 2016 North Carolina Governor Pat McCrory signed into law a bill that bars local governments from passing anti-discrimination protections for lgbtq people.[17]

At their best, federal and state laws that support transgender rights are helpful, and provide some protections at an abstract level. Truthfully, they do not and cannot protect transgender individuals, couples, and communities at the most personal levels of life. Recent examples are found in these very different stories. The first is the annual International Transgender Day of Remembrance, which began as a local event.[18] Despite gains in legal protections in countries such as the United States, the Reading of Names observance list, read at public Memorial Services in 2016 was the longest since these services originated in 1999. Brazil continues to rank number one in the number of transgender persons murdered annually.[19] Mexico ranks second and the United States third in the number of persons murdered as a direct result of either perceived or known transgender identity.

15. CBS News Online, "California Law Allows Transgender Students to Pick Bathrooms, Sports Teams, They Identify With," http://www.cbsnews.com/news/california-law-allows-transgender-students-to-pick-bathrooms-sports-teams-they-identify-with/.

16. Gray, "Exclusion of Transgender People Threatens Rights Bill," November 3, 2014, www.freep.com/story/news/local/michigan/2014/11/12/.

17. Domonoske, "North Carolina Passes Law Blocking Measures to Protect LGBT People," March 24, 2016, http://www.npr.org/sections/thetwo-way/2016/03/24/471700323/north-carolina-passes-law-blocking-measures-to-protect-lgbt-people/.

18. Transgender Day of Remembrance was founded in 1999 by Gwendolyn Ann Smith, a transgender woman, to memorialize the murder of Rita Hester in Allston, Massachusetts. It has evolved from a web-based project and local memorial started by Smith into an international day of action.

19. TGEU Transgender Europe, "Trans Murder Monitoring 2015," May 8, 2015 www.tgeu.org/tmm-idahot-update-2015/.

In most cases, these murders are horrific in brutality. In 2015 in the U.S., one nineteen-year-old transgender individual was chained to a motorcycle and dragged to death; another, a high-school student, was set on fire while traveling on a bus in California.[20] At least three transgender persons were killed in the United States because of their gender identity between Election Day, 2016 and the end of November.

Transphobia and hatred toward transgender persons is not restricted to physical violence. Many who identify as transgender endure a lifetime of isolation, poverty, loneliness; and often rejection by family, friends, and faith community. When I publicly shared my transgender story,[21] I was inundated with emails, letters, and phone calls from other transgender persons who contacted me, sharing personal stories of rejection and persecution. Among these were many responses from persons wanting to share personal spiritual stories and relate both positive and painful experiences in faith-based communities. Many of these communications were laments; tragic stories of rejection by faith communities in which these persons were previously welcome, or even served in leadership. Some stories came from clergy serving stealth (secretly) in congregations or denominations not open to transgender clergy. Many expressed fears that their congregations or denominational authorities would reject them if their gender identity and history became known.

One story shared with me came from a devout Christian I will call Pat. I met Pat after her medical transition. At the time, Pat was living stealth. She had a full-time job in a field she loved and did not want to risk discrimination and possible unemployment if her history became known. A conservative Christian, Pat had been very active in the church as a young adult male with a growing family. Pat served on committees, led Bible studies, and worked with youth groups, and young married couples. One of the events in which Pat most enjoyed participating was the congregation's annual production of The Passion story. Pat had played the role of Judas for several years. People from all around the community came to view the program, and each year's production was featured on the church website until the following season. For the years Pat participated in this event Pat's family were viewed as model Christians, strong lay leaders in their church,

---

20. GLAAD, "Transgender Day of Remembrance Resource Kit for Journalists,"www. glaad.org/publications/tdorkit.

21. Christine McFadden, "Minister Kept Secret for 27 Years," September 1, 2009, http:// www.shermanswilderness.org/the-portland-tribune-minister-kept-secret-for-27-years.

and happily married. What no-one in the congregation knew was that the ideal young family so involved in the community was not as stable and peaceful underneath as they appeared in public. For years Pat had struggled with gender identity issues, always burying them and turning to Christian fundamental theology for strength and help. Like many others who attempt to repress gender identity conflicts, pressure eventually mounted beyond Pat's ability to cope and suicide became the only viable option Pat could see. At this point a crisis occurred for Pat, Pat's spouse, and family.

With the assistance of a therapist grounded in gender identity theory and counseling, Pat began the process of physical transition to the woman she experienced deep within. This was unacceptable to Pat's spouse, whose theological beliefs and church did not support those who identify as transgender. The marriage ended. Pat's spouse declared Pat a deviant sinner, and withdrew all communication and support, taking the rest of Pat's family with her. Pat's pastor and faith community rejected Pat as well. Citing select passages of Scripture, they drove Pat from the community with accusations of perversion and rebellion against God. As Pat shared this story with me, she went to the website of her former church to show me pictures from a Passion story production in which Pat had played Judas. Pat had looked at it only a few months earlier. This time, when she went to the site to show me, Pat's pictures were gone. Judas was erased from the production, from the website, and from the memory of that congregation.

Pat's experience is common and not confined to theologically conservative Christians and congregations. A visitor to my congregation told me of her three most recent experiences attempting to find a faith community near her home. She knew of my transgender history and had traveled a long distance to attend worship and visit afterward. During our conversation, she shared that each of the three faith communities visited declared in some public way that it was welcoming of all persons. But in these congregations, official statements of welcome did not evolve into practice. In one instance, when she asked to participate in the women's group, she was told that was not possible. In another case, following a period of regular attendance in worship and other activities, this person asked to participate in lay leadership opportunities, particularly worship. The church council made it clear she was no longer welcome. The last congregation was even more direct. After three visits the pastor called and told her she made too many members of the church uncomfortable, and they also had no appropriate restroom for her.

In addition to facing violence, rejection, discrimination, chronic unemployment, under-employment, and lack of significant services like safe and affordable health care, transgender persons live each day with the "what if" scenario: what if my employer finds out my background, what if I need medical treatment, what if my family rejects me as I speak out about who I am?

There are no easy answers to such questions, but the 2012 and 2015 surveys from the National Center for Transgender Equality indicates ongoing broad discrimination based on gender identity. Survey results from New England indicated high levels of discrimination, harassment, and resultant economic instability and poverty:

1. *Workplace Discrimination* in the form of mistreatment or harassment: 91%. Loss of job: 21%

2. *Discrimination at school*: reported verbal assault: 81%. Reported physical assault: 34%. Reported sexual assault: 13%

3. *Health Care Discrimination*: reported being refused treatment on basis of transgender identity: 15%. Postponed care because of fear of health care system, lack of insurance or both: 27%

4. *Poverty*: reported annual household income under $10,000.00:13%. This is more than three times the national rate of poverty.

5. *Suicide*: reported attempting suicide: 36%. This is 22 times higher than the general population.[22]

For some, disrespect, denial of transgender identity and violence does not end even in death. In 2014, 26-year-old Idaho resident Jennifer Gable, who worked for Wells Fargo as a customer service coordinator, died suddenly of an aneurysm. Friends attending her open-casket funeral were shocked and dismayed to find her presented as a man. Jennifer was dressed in a suit; her long hair cut off. Meghan Stabler of the Human Rights Campaign, who had previously helped Jennifer commented, "No mention of the woman she knew she was and had lived as for several years. Just erosion of her identity and an old photograph of how the father perceived her to be. She had done what she needed to do legally to be seen as her authentic self. Her father erased her identity either through ignorance or arrogance."[23] The

22. Grant et al. *"National Transgender Discrimination Survey"*, acceshttp://www.transequality.org/issues/national-transgender-discrimination-survey/

23. Rothaus, "Transgender Woman Dies Suddenly, Presented at Funeral in Open

obituary posted by the family also ignored her identity, choosing instead to use male pronouns throughout the obituary and making no reference to her gender identity. Jennifer's story has led more than one transgender acquaintance to revisit their will to make certain this cannot happen to them.

As the stories of Pat, the visitor to my church, and Jennifer all illustrate, the violence, oppression, and cultural marginalization transgender persons endure is often validated and encouraged by the very faith communities to which they turn for protection, comfort, and help.[24] As the conversation with our visitor revealed, this mistreatment and spiritual abuse occurs even in faith communities that openly declare they are welcoming and safe communities.

Two common elements that run through the stories I heard and that align with my own experience as a transgender person are: 1. Unexamined psychological assumptions about human sexuality and gender identity. For example, it is very common for those with little or no education regarding gender identity and/or sexual orientation to confuse and conflate the two. This leads to misperceptions and often the lumping together of policies and programs under the "lgbtq" umbrella. For example, generally whatever ministry programs may exist are often solely focused on sexual orientation issues, never addressing the daily experience and needs of those who identify as transgender. 2. Theological assumptions about the male nature of God can lead to worship and liturgy that is so male-dominant, gender-binary, and exclusive in language that it is uncomfortable or even impossible for transgender persons to enter into worship. A related problem is the absence of education about gender identity, and, consequently how to create a proactive ministry that involves transgender persons in the life of the congregation. Such involvement may include things such as participating with a worship planning group to create inclusive liturgy, Scripture readings, and other resources; or working with the educational program and outreach groups to become more inclusive in program and resource materials.

As the National Transgender Discrimination Survey reveals, the suicide rate among the transgender community is 41% compared to 1.6% for the general public. For a faith-community to offer genuine hospitality and

---

Casket as a Man," March 14, 2014, http://www.miamiherald.com/news/local/community/gay-south-florida/article4055600.html/.

24. Raushenbush, "Christians Are a Cause of LGBT Oppression So We Have to Be a Part of the Liberation!" January 27, 2013, http://www.huffingtonpost.com/paul-raushenbush/christians-lgbt-rights_b_4794753.html.

welcome through welcoming, practical acts of ministry may help many move from isolation into community and a sense of hope. Such ministry could help change these dire statistics. For example, transgender persons are more likely to be unemployed, homeless or living in poverty than the general population: sometimes a meal and safe place for conversation could help address a dire need.

Rethinking worship is a significant form of welcome. How often does the liturgy, music or other parts of the service lift or include those who are transgender? What theological message is given by the pastor regarding gender identity? Does the congregation's ministry include rituals such as Naming Ceremonies, Baptism, or other significant spiritual life events and rituals for transgender persons? Does the congregation offer or participate in the International Transgender Day of Remembrance service, or in local Gay Pride events?

Education and advocacy is another essential ministry. As the visitor to our church had experienced in three previous congregations, many include a sign and official statement of welcome directed specifically to lgbtq people, but not all enact concrete policies, procedures, and protections for their transgender visitors. Even fewer offer practical ministry in the forms of inclusive worship, educational or spiritual growth opportunities, gender-neutral restrooms, or lay leadership opportunities. Beyond actions within the local congregation, many towns and cities include advocacy organizations for transgender persons. A congregation may become active in an advocacy group addressing the needs of transgender and gender non-conforming people in any number of areas.

Spiritual care is crucial for those who have experienced rejection and spiritual abuse in other places, sometimes even among family and close friends. It is critical for a congregation to ask and address questions of the spiritual suffering of transgender persons who have endured spiritual abuse at the hands of families, faith communities, or denomination. Without addressing this spiritual core other gestures, though helpful and hopeful, are inadequate. Spiritually broken people need opportunities for healing; spiritually abused persons need opportunities to hear a different message, to tell their stories, form genuine, safe community and rebuild trust in both God and humankind.

Faith communities could provide a safe and welcoming space for transgender and gender non-conforming people. Drawing again upon Jesus' story of The Good Samaritan, a congregation may offer spiritual,

emotional, and material support by offering a healing space, authentic relationships, and practical acts of hospitality. These elements can help ameliorate past wounds and contribute to present and future well-being. The
following chapters develop the theological foundations for such ministry
and offers one practical model that begins to explore unique aspects and
shared experiences of transgender spirituality. This model takes place within the positive framework of a retreat setting. The retreat described took
place in August of 2015 at The Walker Center in Auburndale, Massachusetts. Attracting persons from nearby as well as other states, the high level
of participation and enthusiasm displayed, as well as written evaluations
provided by the participants, bear witness that such intentional opportunities for transgender communities to gather can be healing and restorative.
As this chapter clearly portrays opportunities for transgender persons to
get together, share stories, and relax in a safe space are too rare.

3

A Theology and Practice of Radical Love

The teaching and practices of Jesus demonstrating the radical nature of divine love point toward a theology that reflects this fundamental instruction. Queer theology may be helpful to inform the connections between transgender and gender non-conforming persons seeking positive spiritual practices and faith communities seeking to develop such ministries. In this chapter I will provide a brief overview of queer theology as it applies to God as Radical Love; and texts from the discipline of spiritual direction that describe methods for actively engaging with others through spiritual practices such as "Holy Listening" and companionship as described by Margaret Guenther.[1] God as Radical Love reflects Jesus' teaching in The Parable of the Good Samaritan and provides a theological bridge that points toward a new model of ministry with and for transgender and gender non-conforming persons. The chapter moves from the broadest topic, Queer Theology, to spiritual guidance and practices that specifically relate to creating safe spaces in which to explore spirituality within a transgender or gender non-conforming framework. The roots of the concept of radical love are found in theological and philosophical discourse. The Book of Ruth and the Parable of the Good Samaritan are often cited as paradigms for this kind of unconditional love that pursues the wellbeing of others. This is a positive theology in its most general form, but when considered in relation to transgender and gender non-conforming persons, who are often confronted with condemnatory theologies, it can be life-saving. Within the

1. Guenther, *Holy Listening: The Art of Spiritual Direction,* Modeling, teaching and practicing the skills of holy listening and companionship in Guenther's book in a retreat setting not only facilitated other retreat activities but became a positive spiritual practice itself.

discipline of Queer Theology, no author moves from the theological concept of Radical Love to personal beliefs and practices that foster spiritual health and healing more clearly than Patrick S. Cheng.

Queer theologian and author Patrick S. Cheng is well-known for his work with lgbtq theology. In his text, *Radical Love: An Introduction to Queer Theology,* Dr. Cheng presents an introduction to Queer theology in combination with God as Radical Love. Cheng's queer Trinitarian theology describes God as "coming out" to humankind and creation through a self-revelation that Cheng terms "Radical Love."[2] God as Radical Love is expressed through the modalities of creation, Word, and human reason, particularly when we employ reason to work back to a first cause.[3] The first cause is God, and all that has been or will be revealed about God points toward an extreme love. This love is so extreme that all known human boundaries are dissolved, and the gap between human and divine is bridged.[4] Within this framework sin is understood as refusing to embrace and engage Radical Love, and continuing to maintain artificial boundaries that divide and oppress.[5] Jesus, the second manifestation of the Trinity is the bridge, embodied revelation, and recovery of Radical Love. Dr. Cheng relates this directly to lgbtq persons:

> Jesus Christ can be understood by LGBT people as the embodiment of Radical Love, or radical love made flesh. As noted in the first chapter of the Gospel according to John, the 'Word became flesh and lived among us.' Indeed, God loved the world so much that God became human in the person of Jesus Christ. If radical love is understood as a love so extreme that it dissolves boundaries, then Jesus Christ is the living embodiment of the dissolution of boundaries. As such, Jesus Christ is the boundary-crosser extraordinaire, whether this relates to divine, social, sexual, or gender boundaries.[6]

This theological perspective suggests that an important dimension of spiritual work for transgender and gender non-conforming persons is to accept this love and to become an authentic witness and expression of this love, particularly when challenging oppression. As persons of faith and

2. Cheng, *Radical Love,* 45.

3. Cheng, 50.

4. Cheng, 50–51.

5. Ibid., 70.

6. Ibid., 79.

persons whose identity expression challenges current cultural boundaries, transgender persons are also called to challenge the boundaries that Jesus challenged, including the transgression of social boundaries that enforce or support oppression and violence towards others.[7]

Beyond a discussion of God as Radical Love, and the challenge made to lgbtq persons to accept and embody this love in our lives, specific suggestions and sources of support are needed. Patrick Cheng remarks that it is through pastoral care and church communities that lgbtq people move from isolation into communities of radical love.[8]

In his 2003 book *Transgendered: Theology, Ministry, and Communities of Faith,* Justin Tanis also addresses the significance of understanding the radical love of God and embracing all that God has created each person to become.[9] Like Cheng, Tanis connects the embodiment of this love with the person of Jesus, and describes Jesus as one who transgressed many cultural boundaries, including gender.[10] Tanis' focus is specifically transgender persons, and he encourages transgender followers of Jesus to seek out a safe spiritual community in which to practice a healthy spirituality.

In a chapter exploring creating genuine welcome and hospitality for transgender people Dr. Tanis presents a more detailed description of the fear many transgender persons experience even when thinking about visiting a faith community. He also includes the fears sometimes voiced by gay, lesbian, and bisexual members of a congregation who may worry that transgender people are still socially marginalized and will somehow adversely affect whatever gains they have already made.[11] Justin Tanis thus lifts up some of the particular experiences and issues faced by transgender people seeking safe spaces for spiritual community. This addition is important to any conversation about creating welcome and providing ministry to those who identify as transgender or gender non-conforming.

Early in this text, Tanis paints a powerful image of a dilemma faced by transgender children who know themselves to be different. This is a dilemma that affects every aspect of what it means to be human: physical, psychological, and spiritual:

7. Ibid., 80.
8. Ibid., 112.
9. Tanis, *Transgendered*, 145.
10. Ibid., 138–139.
11. Ibid., 116–117.

Transgender children face a horrifying dilemma of hiding what they know about themselves until they reach adulthood or being honest and facing the risks of being thrown out of the family home or punished at home, church or school with repeated violence. Profound spiritual violence is wrought on an individual for hiding the truth of him-or herself or facing human hostility year after year.[12]

Such abuses can have a profound impact on a personal sense of relationship with God, instill experiences of shame, and discourage a person's willingness or ability to seek a faith community in which to learn to trust, heal, and grow.

Perhaps because of his own life experience as a transgender man, Justin Tanis includes a chapter in his book that covers gender variance and Scripture.[13] For Tanis, God does create distinctions from the beginning, but these are not solid boundaries and total opposites. From the beginning, these spaces overlap in what Tanis defines as "liminal spaces" in which the elements of creation overlap and merge.[14] Surely the same could be said about the creation of humanity with people occupying many places between the poles of female and male in a way similar to the rest of creation.[15] Throughout this section Tanis provides several examples of Scripture passages that address gender variance and provides exegetical work relevant to transgender and gender non-conforming persons. This section may be especially encouraging and beneficial for transgender persons who have experienced spiritual abuse through the misinterpretation and/or misapplication of certain Scriptures in the past.

In one example of trans-positive scripture passages Tanis offers an exegesis of Matthew 19:11–12:

> But Jesus said to the disciples, "Not everyone can accept this teaching, but only those to whom it is given. For there are eunuchs who have been so from birth, and there are eunuchs who have been made eunuchs by others, and there are eunuchs who have made themselves eunuchs for the sake of the dominion of heaven. Let anyone accept this who can."

12. Tanis, 33.

13. Ibid., 55–84.

14. For an extensive discussion of gender-fluid theology and a gender continuum see Virginia Ramey Mollenkott, *Omnigender*.

15. Ibid., 58.

For Tanis, Eunuchs are the closest analogy in Scripture to transgender people.[16] In his exegesis of this text he suggests that Jesus' teaching regarding eunuchs reveals his acceptance of gender-variant people, including those today who identify as transgender.[17] Based upon this and other texts Tanis concurs with what Patrick Cheng states more broadly about lgbtq persons; that the process of self-acceptance (grounded in God as Radical Love) is essential for the spiritual health and well-being of transgender people.[18]

Justin Tanis and Patrick Cheng both offer positive theological resources for those who identify as transgender or gender variant. These texts are helpful educational resources for faith communities as well. Tanis' book in particular offers a series of practical steps covering topics such as full inclusion of transgender persons in the life of the church, education of the congregation, and restroom provisions and policies.[19]

Tanis moves beyond Cheng to make a theological distinction between transgender persons and lesbian, gay, and bisexual people. Referencing and quoting Tanis regarding Jesus as one who crossed gender boundaries, Patrick Cheng notes how Tanis draws parallels between the life of Jesus and many life events transgender persons experience: bullying and harassment, social rejection, homelessness, and physical violence.[20]

Tanis draws an existential parallel between those transgender persons who choose to medically transition with participation in the experience of resurrection.[21] This comparison is a powerful and provocative theological statement offered to transgender and gender variant persons. It also provides one reason for distinguishing transgender from the broader lesbian, gay, and bisexual umbrella in terms of ministry. Tanis discusses medical transition in relation to Christology and the resurrection:

> Jesus' example may guide us to a healthy way of looking at this transformation. Jesus' body was changed, both by becoming alive after death and in ways that made him appear different to those who knew him; at the same time, he was the same Jesus who had been among them, as Jesus' revelation to Thomas shows. Here Jesus is careful to make the point that he is both the same and

16. Tanis, 69.
17. Ibid., 74–75.
18. Tanis, 74.
19. Ibid., 115–128.
20. Ibid., 83.
21. Tanis, 83.

different, which is true of us as well. Jesus did not die and return
as a wholly different being but as a transfigured and resurrected
one. In this way, Jesus is a trans person, both through his personal
transformations in body and spirit, and in the ways in which he
embodies, transcends, and defies categorization.[22]

It is important to note that Justin Tanis is not equating the unique
resurrection of Jesus as the Christ with the experience of transgender persons. The resurrection recorded in Scripture is unique to Jesus. The point
is that the experience of physical transformation, of being different yet the
same, of defying gender-binary categorization differentiates transgender
and gender non-conforming persons from the sexual orientation issues
and foci of gay, lesbian, and bisexual people and communities. This is true
whether or not one chooses to medically transition. For transgender and
gender non-conforming people, authentically embracing one's true gender
identity generates the rebirth experience. Not all transgender and gender
non-conforming persons choose to medically transition, but many describe
"coming out" as the beginning of a new life. Persons often choose biblical
and other spiritual stories and images of transformation and resurrection
to express their own sense of rebirth.

There are gay, lesbian, and bisexual transgender and gender non-conforming persons, but gender-identity is the common, primary experience
shared by this population. It is this experience that fundamentally affects
how one understands, experiences, perceives, and embodies the world.
This existential situation results in unique needs and concerns in terms
of faith communities and spiritual practices. This certainly does not mean
that transgender people cannot benefit from simply being part of a broader
faith community, or find it valuable to participate in lgbtq programs and
events. However, there is a particular practice that is essential for many
who identify as transgender and gender non-conforming: to have safe time
and space to deal with issues unique to this experience. For example, the in-
congruity between physical body and gender identity experienced by most
who identify as transgender is not generally addressed either in general
faith-based programs or events focused on sexual orientation.

Many transgender and gender non-conforming persons were forced
to wear clothing perceived as inappropriate; were socialized and forced
to interact primarily with the wrong peer-group; and have experienced
verbal if not physical abuse from others for apparent transgression of

22. Ibid., 142–43.

socio-religious norms around gender performance and identity. This history alone illustrates the need for time, space, and tools to process these experiences for spiritual healing and growth.

Being or becoming a genuinely welcoming faith community is a substantial positive step in offering healing and wholeness both to transgender persons and to members of faith communities who are currently transphobic. Establishing authentic relationships with those we fear or view as "other" is a critical step toward the unbounded love described by Jesus in The Parable of the Good Samaritan. Conversations on the topic of welcoming transgender persons continue to grow. For example, in January 2016 retired Episcopal Bishop Eugene Robinson published a report through the Center for American Progress that argues in favor of welcoming transgender and gender non-conforming persons into faith communities.[23] In addition to such educational reports, Cheng, Tanis and others offer educational, programmatic, and practical resources for becoming more hospitable and welcoming. This resource aims to expand these resources to include the intentional development of safe time and space for transgender and gender non-conforming persons to gather together and engage in practices and conversations pertinent to the unique aspects of being transgender.

Accepting the image of God as radical, all-inclusive love, as depicted through the theology of Patrick Cheng; Justin Tanis' call to authenticity; and ongoing conversations about welcome such as the report presented by Bishop Gene Robinson, point toward a common spiritually healthy response on the part of transgender and gender non-conforming persons: self-acceptance and choosing to live authentically in life. Spiritual practices that support this choice are vital to this process.

In the Christian tradition, there is a long history of seeking to connect with God and to live authentically in the world. From earliest roots in the birth of the Monastic movement in second century Egypt, many practices and methods for spiritual growth have developed over the centuries.[24] Today, practices such as spiritual direction, meditation, and retreats are engaged by many persons of faith seeking to connect more closely with God and to live authentically in the world. Such opportunities, especially retreats, are

---

23. Robinson, "*Transgender Welcome: A Bishop Makes the Case for Affirmation*," January 19, 2016, https://www.americanprogress.org/issues/religion/report/2016/01/19/129101/transgender-welcome/.

24. Swan, *The Forgotten Desert Mothers*, 21.

limited or virtually non-existent for those who identify as transgender or gender non-conforming.

Many nonspecific spiritual direction, meditation classes, and retreat opportunities certainly are meant to be helpful for and welcoming to those who identify as transgender people. I have participated in many such events and often leave with a sense of renewal and recommitment. But broad, inclusive gatherings are limited. They generally do not address Queer Theology, explore the spiritual depths of living in the world as a transgender or gender non-conforming person, or provide a sense of safety necessary for deep sharing. There may be only one transgender person present, unintentionally creating an atmosphere that causes that person to feel more vulnerable and isolated. In such a setting, it is not unusual for gender non-conforming members to withdraw.[25]

Safety and trust are core for transgender persons. Growing up exposed to bullying and abuse as many are, leads some persons to withdraw and isolate, only leaving the relative safety of home when absolutely necessary. Expulsion from family and faith communities because of gender identity leaves some afraid to build new relationships. The daily stress of life as a transgender person within a culture that mocks, discriminates against and too often physically brutalizes transgender people sometimes results in physical, emotional, and spiritual exhaustion. All of them raise the threshold for feeling genuinely safe, or the willingness to invest in trusting another person or community. Opportunities like small group retreats provide a place where some rebuilding of trust and sense of safety may take place in the midst of positive spiritual practices. This process of rebuilding trust is essential for the response to Radical Love Cheng envisions, the authenticity embraced by Tanis, and honest participation in welcoming communities of faith.

Providing a welcoming and safe space and time for theological conversation and new or renewed exploration of spiritual practices requires spiritual guidance. Like Patrick Cheng, Spiritual Director Peg Thompson writes about the coming out process in spiritual direction, and the deeply spiritual nature of this process. While she limits her focus to gay, lesbian, and bisexual persons, her description of key stages and spiritual turning-points are applicable to the transgender community, particularly in her conclusion:

25. Law, *The Wolf Shall Dwell with the Lamb*, 1–10.

> Coming out almost invariably involves spiritual and religious issues. It asks us to reevaluate and reposition ourselves in relation to religion-doctrine, scripture, community, clergy-and spirituality-integrity, prayer, images of God, relationship with the sacred. At every step there are choices to be made, choices that fundamentally alter the course of the interior life as well as the exterior.[26]

Providing transgender persons with opportunities to engage such spiritual work moves beyond building, program, and educational issues of welcome and including transgender members in a faith community. It is also more specific and focused than an lgbtq or general gathering can be or become. This is a specific and practical outreach ministry dedicated to the healing and renewal of a population often wounded by others professing to speak for God and/or the Church.

In her book chapter, "The Coming Out Process in Spiritual Direction," Thompson identifies six stages in this process for gay and lesbian persons: awareness of differentness, identity confusion, acceptance, identity assumption, affirmation and celebration, and activism.[27] While not identical neither are these stages dissimilar to the stages many transgender people experience. As Thompson notes regarding those who identify as gay or lesbian, the process of coming out never ends. This is true for transgender and gender non-conforming people as well. Transgender persons must deal with coming out many times over a lifetime. Some examples include employment, health care, housing and neighbors, faith community, activism, new friends and personal relationships. In every case there are emotions and unfinished issues that may resurface, creating a need to revisit past assumptions and current life situation. There are also occasions when persons living stealth (i.e. not public regarding their gender identity) may become weary of the stress of keeping such a significant part of one's self hidden, or the constant underlying anxiety of being "outed" by someone else. For transgender and gender non-conforming persons there is also the pressure and stress of increasing violence towards members of our community from within the broader society. There are intense political struggles over issues such as public restrooms, appropriate locker rooms for transgender students, and whether or not the transgender community is entitled to equal protections in areas such as employment, housing, and health care. These

26. Thompson, "The Coming Out Process in Spiritual Direction," in *Spiritual Direction in Context*, Nick Wagner, ed., 120.

27. Thompson, 111–119.

experiences and stressors can and do lead some to question the presence, love, or existence of God, creating spiritual questioning, or a crisis of faith. Gender identity is a core dimension of human life. When this identity is denied, questioned, or violated it invariably leads to existential and spiritual questions. When faced with relationship, employment, housing, or health issues I have listened to people ask again and again, "Is there a God?", "Did God make me this way?", "Does God hate me/ laugh at me?", "Why does God keep letting this happen?" Because coming out is inextricably connected to spiritual and religious issues, each time a transgender person faces a turning point or event in one of these areas it triggers a reevaluation in every area of life, including our spiritual core.[28] At such times practical ministries such as spiritual direction and exploration can be healing and beneficial in the process of discernment and renewal.

Spiritual Director and Episcopal Priest Margaret Guenther adds the dimension of presence and attentive listening into the conversation. In, *Holy Listening: The Art of Spiritual Direction"* she discusses the importance of genuine welcome and hospitality as elements of spiritual companionship. In the act of sharing space, she reflects:

> We invite someone into a space that offers safety and shelter and put our own needs aside, as everything is focused on the comfort and refreshment of the guest. For a little while at least, *mi casa es tu casa*, as the Spanish gracefully puts it. There are provisions for cleansing, food, and rest. Hospitality is an occasion for storytelling with both laughter and tears, and then the guest moves on, perhaps with some extra provisions or a roadmap for the next stage of the journey.[29]

Such a space and time for sharing stories and companionship is invaluable in working with such a marginalized group.

In her article, "Living in the Image of God: Transgender People in Spiritual Direction" Spiritual Director Laura Thor also discusses the importance of companionship, specifically in working with transgender persons:

> Like many directors, I have experienced how the holy work of companioning religiously marginalized and ostracized people is radical in nature: our companionship gives witness and aid to their own holy work of "storming Heaven's gates" to find God where religious institutions and dogmas can't yet seem to grant

28. Wagner, 120.

29. Guenther, *Holy Listening*, 14.

access. So deep is many transgender persons' absorption of negative religious messages that their spiritual work involves a process of birthing the spiritual self; ours as "midwives" is to re-mind our Seekers, and ourselves, that life in all its diversity is welcome in the Divine milieu.[30]

The radical companionship Thor describes includes asking her clients about their dawning childhood awareness of being gender non-conforming, and how they thought about it or tried to express it. This process of sharing life stories is an essential part of spiritual companionship. In response to her question Thor heard stories from some who hoped God did not know, and would never discover how they felt. Others prayed at night and hoped to wake up in the right body. A minority believed God not only knew but made them this way, and would reconcile everything in time.

In Thompson's book chapter the process of spiritual direction in relation to gay and lesbian persons also describes helping people tell their stories, and the story of their lives.[31] Like Thor, she also notes the harm sometimes done by early childhood religious teachings around areas of human sexuality. Changing her language slightly to reference the transgender community, this becomes a significant statement: "When we are companioning (transgender persons) these early teachings-and the feelings that go with them-are a major part of what stands in the way not only of a self-affirming (transgender) identity but of a greater intimacy with the Holy."[32]

It is significant that sharing life stories is foundational in spiritual direction and companionship with transgender and gender non-conforming persons. These are powerful stories when shared with a spiritual companion; but they may be more powerful when shared among a common community. In a setting such as a retreat, facilitators may become companions in sharing significant spiritual stories. Combined with positive theological language provided by Queer theologians such as Patrick Cheng and Justin Tanis, such a retreat may become the framework upon which spiritual and religious reevaluation, discernment, and renewal take place.

30. Thor, "Living in the Image of God: Transgender People in Spiritual Direction" *Presence: An International Journal of Spiritual Direction*, 52–59.

31. Wagner, 112.

32. Wagner, 112–113.

4

Retreating Forward

Context, Content, and Radical Hospitality

The history and current circumstances of transgender and gender non-conforming persons illuminate the need to consider context, content, and radical hospitality in planning ministry with and for this population. In my work these themes emerged through conversations with other transgender and gender non-conforming persons, and research, such as survey questions, related to creating the retreat later described. In light of the findings of an initial questionnaire and email communications with the group interested in participating in a retreat, a decision was made to focus the retreat on spiritual practices, especially spiritual autobiography, and hospitality. These key features are all important to facilitate healing and renewal within the transgender and gender non-conforming community. This chapter will explore each theme in relation to its part in the formation of a retreat.

The contexts in which transgender people live are challenging at many levels, but one of the most devastating is social isolation; they often have few opportunities to experience hospitality. As surveys indicate and personal stories confirm, transgender people are often forced or required to deny, suppress, or otherwise ignore their authentic life stories to survive on even a basic level. This may begin at a very young age, especially within families and communities in which gender identity is not tolerated as a topic of discussion or debate. Whether the suppression is grounded in efforts to earn love and approval, fear of rejection and isolation from family and friends, or something else entirely, transgender people often endure long periods of time concealing their authentic self from others. This is isolating and often socially and spiritually debilitating.

I grew up in an earlier and more isolated era. Although the 1960's was a time of radical change and increasing social liberalism, most had never heard about gender identity or what was then known as transsexualism. Although my nuclear family was not rigidly structured around gender roles, the community in which I lived was very conservative. The public-school system especially became a place first of struggle, then protest, and finally increasing silence for me. Bullied by teachers, staff, and peers I initially protested verbally and vigorously over pronouns, dress codes, and especially enforced participation in Home Economics and gym class. After countless hours spent in the vice-principal's office for a variety of offenses, including a three-day suspension for inappropriate dress, I grew increasingly withdrawn. At that time, there were no support groups for lgbtq students, no education about either sexual orientation or gender identity. There was also no internet or social network support.

When I began the process of medical transition as a young adult in Cleveland, Ohio, I was encouraged by my physicians and other professional staff to invent a history, ostensibly for my own safety and protection. I did not like the idea. I remember arguing in particular with a psychiatrist over the question of whether honesty was not always the best policy. I believed it was. However, after a few negative experiences of sharing my history with new friends or potential dating partners I began to understand why I had been advised to refrain from talking about the past. While there were many positive responses, the negative and painful ones reinforced powerful messages from childhood about self-esteem and worth. These negative experiences overshadowed the positive ones, and I grew increasingly selective about the people with whom I shared my history. This was like the earlier silence I experienced in school, except that now it was a silence of my own creation.

For twenty-eight years, very few of those closest to me in life knew my whole self. This included family members, friends, colleagues, and most members of the communities in which I lived. The exceptions were my spouse, a few who had known me most of my life, my physician, and select friends. While this life appeared basically successful and conventional on the outside, the cost of living with so much that was unspoken, unshared, and unembraced by community at an authentic level became increasingly intolerable for me. For these and other reasons I moved from silence to publicly sharing my life story in 2009. While the results of that decision are not the subject of this text, it is relevant that despite difficulties, the benefits of authenticity far outweigh any costs.

Tangible progress has been made during the decades following the sixties in terms of visibility, research and education, and civil rights advocacy and protections for transgender persons; however, bullying, shaming, and violence continue. With every legal protection and victory gained has come a backlash of verbal and physical aggression, as evidenced by the increasing number of known victims named every year during Transgender Day of Remembrance ceremonies. In 2015, twenty-one persons were reported as victims of fatal violence in the United States. This is the largest number on record for any year.[1] By November of 2016 at least twenty-two transgender persons were reported as victims of violent crime. This increasing violence understandably causes many transgender and gender non-conforming persons to hide their authentic identity and life stories from others.

This practice, known as living "stealth," carries consequences. For some, living stealth, and never sharing or acknowledging one's past or the consequences of being transgender, is a very conscious decision. Others find their earlier history and life stories stripped from them through the rejection of family, faith community, friends, and colleagues. In extreme cases children are expelled from home and every form of security, family photos are altered to remove any evidence of the "former" member; and persons once known as colleagues or friends stop communicating.

Such personal erasure and rejection can be emotionally damaging and spiritually painful when it comes from one's faith community. One powerful example of such rejection is the story of Pat told in chapter 2, whose annual participation in "The Passion Story" production of her faith community was literally erased from the website of the church she attended after she was forced to leave. Whether imposed from without or from within, living "stealth" costs transgender persons fundamental human connections, a sense of place, and connection with their life history; as memories go unshared and stories untold. One result of such forced and prolonged suppression may be a deep spiritual and human need to share forgotten or fragmented life stories with themselves, and their families, friends, and wider community.

---

1. "Global Resources," Transgender Europe, May 8, 2015, http://tgeu.org/resources/global-resources/.

Some transgender persons engage this desire to share their stories in the form of education, speaking to individuals, groups and organizations in hopes of abating current negative attitudes, laws, and behaviors towards the transgender community; and creating a better future for following generations of transgender and gender non-conforming people. Others describe sharing life stories as a more private and personal journey, one form of self-expression and sharing authenticity. Most speak of remembering and sharing their stories as a way to make sense of the world, and of being a transgender person living within this world.

Existential analysis of the meaning of life is spiritual in nature. As Viktor Frankl notes, people respond to life through the process of meaning-making. At some point, such meaning-making moves into the realm of belief:

> In contrast to what people are prone to assume, namely, believing is not at all some sort of thinking *minus* the *reality* of that which is thought, believing is rather some sort of thinking *plus* something, namely, the *existentiality* of him or her who does the thinking.[2]

Because many if not most transgender stories are related to authenticity and existential questions, they can be described as spiritual autobiographies. This fact guided the development of content for the retreat. A retreat that offers time, safe space, basic needs, and a process and structure to write and share spiritual autobiographies may help transgender and gender non-conforming persons with healing, renewal, and the development of future spiritual practices. Such a retreat setting also provides time, space, and conversation for the formation of a transgender-positive theological framework, replacing older models based upon proof-texting, judgment, and shame. The fundamental theological question is how may the message of the Bible, particularly the gospel incarnated in Jesus, become good news for those who are transgender.[3]

The history of writing and sharing spiritual autobiographic content is long and varied. Many spiritual classics contain such elements. For example, both the Quran (containing the sacred writings of Islam) and The Bhagavad Gita (a sacred spiritual story for Hindus) contain elements of spiritual autobiography in describing the relationship with the Sacred. This is true in the Christian tradition as well and is the focus in this chapter and project.

2. Frankl, *Man's Search for Ultimate Meaning*, 146.

3. Phan, *Journeys at the Margins: Toward an Autobiographical Theology in American-Asian Perspective*, xvi.

The collected sayings of the Desert Fathers and Mothers, early Christian theological works such as the Confessions of Augustine, medieval mystical testimonies as revealed by Julian of Norwich, and the recorded stories of African-American women spiritual leaders of the nineteenth century provide examples of the long tradition of this practice. Stories of personal revelation and spiritual journeys are recorded in every Christian era and culture.[4]

Despite such a rich and extensive history, many who identify as Christian know little or nothing about such writings and what they reveal about Christian spirituality, mysticism, and experience of the Sacred. Attending worship, perhaps a Sunday school class or Adult Bible study, and the exercise of personal prayer are the typical observances of many practicing Christians today. The interpretation of Scripture texts presented in sermons and Sunday school curriculum is often the basis of personal faith. This type of assimilated faith might sustain many Christians over a lifetime. Problems can and often emerge, however, when the precepts and interpretations one learned begin to break down over pressing existential questions grounded in personal experience. Additional issues also emerge for transgender persons when their family and/or faith community rejects them because of gender identity and expression. Faced with questions about faith and gender identity, the discovery and exploration of lesser well-known spiritual autobiographical texts may provide a fresh and more constructive spiritual framework.

Julian of Norwich, a 14th century Christian mystic who lived in Norwich, England as an enclosed anchoress attached to the church of St. Julian in Conisford at Norwich, provides one example.[5] During this period of time, Julian recorded a series of sixteen revelations, or "showings," given to her by God. Two fundamental principles revealed in these showings may be of great benefit and comfort to transgender persons: 1. Describing Jesus as Mother and using gender-fluid language in describing the relationships within the Trinity, and 2. Describing the essential nature of God as unconditional love.

For transgender and gender non-conforming persons raised in a conservative patriarchal church, the experience of hearing God described

4. Swan, *The Forgotten Desert Mothers: Sayings, Lives, and Stories of Early Christian Women* (New York: Paulist Press, 2001); Augustine, *Confessions of St. Augustine*, http://www.ccel.org/ccel/augustine/confess.html/; Julian of Norwich, *Showings*, Colledge and James Walsh, trans; Andrews, *Sisters of the Spirit*.

5. Julian, 18.

in feminine terms with qualities of motherly love is a new experience. In my work this proved true even for those raised in theologically progressive faith communities. The participants found it refreshing and reinforcing to hear gender-fluid language for God. Some participants on the retreat shared stories of growing up in households where God was described only in masculine terms and generally portrayed as a judgmental God, particularly around issues of gender roles and human sexuality. Transgender persons familiar with such a background may find the retreat experience especially provocative and healing.

In his preface to *Showings*, J. Leclercq states that the doctrinal issue that makes Julian's writings most timely is her many references to God and Christ as Mother. Leclercq notes that Julian did not invent this language but draws from a long tradition that is relatively unknown today and cites Julian's originality in applying such gender-fluidity to the Trinity.[6] This gender fluid interaction is described in several chapters. A reference from chapter fifty-nine is one brief example:

> So Jesus Christ, who opposes good to evil, is our true Mother. We have our being from him, where the foundation of motherhood begins, with all the sweet protection of love which endlessly follows: As truly as God is our Father, so truly is God our Mother, and he revealed that in everything.[7]

As for the ultimate purpose of sharing her Revelations: "She wants to show that the path of joy is one of quiet humility in sufferings and in consolations, of calm and peace in everything which occurs between souls and their motherly God, their courteous Lord."[8] This is an ultimate purpose with which many transgender and gender non-conforming people can resonate, both in experiences of humility around issues of gender, shame, bullying and isolation; and in the comfort found in community and the support of safe spiritual care.

Strongly connected to a Mothering God and Christ is Julian's showing that describes divine love as the ultimate source and end of all things. She expresses this theological concept first in chapter twenty-seven. As Julian ponders the reason for any sense of separation between herself and God she wonders why sin exists, since it seems to be what prevents people from drawing close to God. In her thirteenth revelation, Jesus responds to her

6. Leclercq, *Showings*, 8–9.

7. Leclercq, *Showings*, 295.

8. Ibid., 20.

query in a vision saying, "Sin is necessary but all will be well, and all will be well, and every kind of thing will be well."[9] This becomes a key theme and point of focus in Julian's visions and writings. She wrestles with questions about sin, evil, and sufferings throughout *Showings*, including her own personal issues and sense of spiritual failures.

Julian believes God has every reason to act harshly towards humans and expresses wonder that instead she experiences a personal, warm, and loving response to her questions, doubts, and fears. Finally, at the very end of her text, she is shown the ultimate meaning of the book and its revelations, which confirms her earlier vision that "all shall be well." These words are found in the final chapter, chapter eighty-six:

> And from the time it was revealed, I desired many times to know in what was our Lord's meaning. And fifteen years after and more, I was answered in spiritual understanding, and it was said: What, do you wish to know your Lord's meaning in this thing? Know it well, love was his meaning. Who reveals this to you? Love. Why does he reveal it to you? For love. Remain in this, and you will know more of the same. But you will never know different, without end.[10]

Despite human sinfulness, brokenness, and evil, God will reconcile all things under the broad umbrella of divine love in the end. This is the kind of unconditional, motherly love of which Julian writes in *Showings*.

Together, Julian's gender-fluid language and her theological doctrine regarding divine love as the beginning and end of all things present a positive language and theological foundation for transgender persons. Participants on the retreat who were unfamiliar with this history of feminine images of God and Jesus did in fact find these ideas freeing and provocative. Some shared similar concepts and/or stories of experiencing God as beyond any gender or gender binary.

Julian of Norwich is one example among many possibilities for exploring transgender-positive theology and imagery. In addition to spiritual autobiographies and classics, there are non-canonical texts that may be useful for personal contemplation in the formation of a transgender positive theology and spiritual practices. One sample comes from the Nag Hammadi Library, a collection of thirteen ancient books discovered in Upper Egypt in 1945. Within this collection is found one short text, "The Thunder: Perfect

---

9. Julian, 224–225.

10. Ibid., 342.

Mind." This text is rich in gender-fluid theological language and imagery. One of several believed destroyed during the struggle to define Christian orthodoxy, the text provides what the authors of, *A New, New Testament: A Bible for the 21st Century Combining Traditional and Newly Discovered Texts* refer to as a "diffuse engenderedness." This engenderedness challenges current standards and values of femininity and masculinity.[11] Here is one short but rich example: "I am the bride and the bridegroom. And it is my husband who gave birth to me. I am my father's mother, my husband's sister, and he is my child."[12]

Such passages contain a wealth of images, meanings and roles on the topic of gender for all persons to think about and discuss, but they may be particularly profound for gender non-conforming people. Editor Hal Tausigg makes this remark about The Thunder: Perfect Mind and gender:

> It offers readers today the chance to identify with Jesus and Thunder without rehearsing and reinforcing the long-held Western ideas of a defended and prescribed femininity and masculinity. Here the twentieth-and twenty-first-century 'queer movements' have much to offer in understanding these ancient portraits and Thunder.[13]

Taussig is correct in stating "queer movements" have much to offer in understanding Thunder. It is also true that *Thunder: Perfect Mind* has much to offer to transgender and gender non-conforming persons in terms of imagery and forming a sense of connection with an ancient spirituality in which gender fluidity plays a significant part.

In addition to the non-canonical texts found in Nag Hammadi there are also scripture texts from the canonical New Testament that provide a framework for theological reflection and conversation around gender identity. The parable of The Good Samaritan offers both transgender and cis-gender persons an opportunity to view the story from the perspective of gender non-conforming persons as neighbor. From this viewpoint it is possible to reflect on transgender persons in both the role of victim and Good Samaritan. Paul's letter to the congregation in Galatia contains another example of a Scripture passage conducive to conversation around gender identity. What might the significance of such verses as Galatians 3:26–29 be for those who identify as transgender: "For you are all sons of God, through

11. Taussig, *A New New Testament*, 180–181.

12. Taussig, 183.

13. Ibid., 181.

your faith in Jesus Christ. For all of you who were baptized into union with Christ clothed yourselves with Christ. There is neither Judean nor Greek, slave nor free, male and female, for in Christ Jesus you are all one"?[14] Conversations around readings such as these can lead to new and fresh insights in developing a positive Christian theology concerning gender identity and in being a transgender follower of Jesus. Such a theological foundation may help guide someone seeking community into a positive and welcoming space.

Texts like these have the potential to evoke images and language for one's own journey, and to inspire the writing and sharing of personal stories. A retreat setting offers ample time and a safe space in which to make connections between sacred writings, the stories of others, and one's personal spiritual journey as a transgender person.

Writing spiritual autobiography has become increasingly popular in recent decades as a practice of spiritual exploration, and may be a healing tool in a retreat setting as participants explore the personal story of God's presence and interaction in their lives. Such writing may be helpful particularly for transgender persons whose previous church or family experience resulted in suppressing positive past experiences, ignoring current spiritual interests or inclinations, or discounting the sacred altogether. Although there are currently no texts that focus on writing spiritual autobiography from a transgender perspective, several basic texts on writing and sharing spiritual autobiography may be helpful to the process.

As Richard Peace notes in, *Spiritual Autobiography: Discovering and Sharing Your Spiritual Story*, one of the greatest benefits of writing spiritual biography is becoming more aware of the active presence of God in life. Peace refers to this growing awareness as "noticing" and comments:

> This is one reason it is so useful to write a spiritual autobiography. It draws the strands of our lives together in a way that points to their meaning; it reminds us of where true reality lies in contrast to the illusions of modern life. A spiritual autobiography encourages us to notice God, and as we notice, our lives are changed.[15]

This practice of noticing God resonates with many transgender persons. Many, like myself re-count an awareness of "God" early in life, and often the awareness is associated with questions and prayers related to gender

---

14. Taussig, 299.

15. Peace, *Spiritual Autobiography*, 58.

and identity. It is not uncommon for a gender non-conforming person to report feelings of being "different," of being "the observer," of viewing life from a perspective unlike many other people. Some describe this experience as spiritual in nature. Reflecting upon and writing personal spiritual autobiography in a retreat setting provides the opportunity to begin this process of connection and supplies tools for continuing the practice when the retreat is over and people return home.

One fundamental difference between a small group of cis-gendered individuals and one of transgender persons focusing on spiritual autobiography concerns the context from which they come and shared life experiences not commonly experienced by the general public. This aspect has an impact on the context, design, and structure of the retreat. For example, in Peace's book he lifts a growing unawareness and complacency as a basic reason people fail to notice God's presence in their lives. He then details how one role of, and reason for, writing and sharing personal spiritual stories is to regain this awareness.[16] While this may also be true for some transgender persons, a more common experience is one of being shut-off from noticing God's activity in life in direct response to the pain and trauma of being ejected from one's family and/or faith community because of gender identity. Factoring this prevalent history into the early content of the retreat may help facilitate a positive experience for some participants by providing an opportunity to express this as well as other aspects of life. Our retreat provided this through an ice-breaker activity involving post-it notes clustered in significant groupings created by participants, and posted on a large wall.

The classic pattern or form for writing spiritual autobiography is concisely defined as a four-part structure by Amy Mandelker and Elizabeth Powers in their introduction to the anthology *Pilgrim Souls: A Collection of Spiritual Autobiographies*. They list these steps as follows: 1. describing one's life prior to spiritual wakening; 2. relating the significant events leading up to this awakening; 3. Describing in detail the encounter with God and the impact of the experience on the narrator; and 4. celebrating the new life experienced because of this episode.[17] Among the transgender community this pattern often coincides with the journey of becoming aware of one's transgender identity. Each story is unique, diverse, and wonderful, yet all

---

16. Peace, 58–59.

17. Mandelker and Powers, eds. *Pilgrim Souls: A Collection of Spiritual Autobiographies*, 16.

share the perspective of a marginalized individual living within a larger marginalized group searching to discover "the salience of the supernatural in the quotidian."[18] A retreat setting where transgender persons may safely share such stories and explore this four-part pattern may itself be a source of spiritual renewal.

Context and content are both essential to consider and carefully plan in facilitating a spiritual retreat for gender non-conforming people. A third theme that is equally important, and is the foundation for the others, is the practice of radical hospitality. The most beautiful, inclusive setting paired with a quality program can fall short of its mark without the presence of what Amy G. Oden defines as "gospel hospitality." Gospel hospitality differs from ordinary, traditional hospitality in depth, width, and willingness to risk surprise and change in offering welcome. While Amy Oden makes this statement as a general reason why this kind of welcome is important and necessary, I find these words especially meaningful and poignant if slightly altered to specifically address transgender persons:

> [Transgender] Spiritual wanderers show up at our doors, not because they like our buildings or even because they like us, but because they are hungry. Hungry for forgiveness, for rest and peace. Hungry for mercy and grace. Hungry to explore and grow. Hungry for the good news of new life, of abundant life. Hungry for God to do a new thing.[19]

The presence and practice of hospitality supports the birth of new ideas and images of God, helping to create a positive experience for participants.[20]

Radical hospitality is modeled after the way God welcomes us; a welcome enfleshed and given voice in and through Jesus. Through Jesus, God not only becomes human, God also invites and hosts humankind in a new form of relationship. The depth and inclusiveness of this welcome is revealed through the life, teaching, death, and resurrection of Jesus. For Oden, as for Julian of Norwich, the foundation of all creation is divine unconditional love.[21] Despite the many stories and references to such welcome contained in Hebrew and New Testament Scriptures, some people never hear this message or experience such a welcome.[22] A retreat grounded in

18. Ibid., 265.

19. Oden, *God's Welcome*, 12.

20. Ibid., 14.

21. Oden, 33.

22. Ibid., 34–37.

the type of hospitality Amy Oden describes as gospel hospitality may allow some persons to receive and practice a depth of welcome not previously experienced. This is true for retreat participants, facilitators, and others involved.

Amy Oden's discussion of four qualities of gospel hospitality are valuable when reflecting upon group dynamics. She cites the story of Abraham and Sarah (Genesis 18:1–5) as the primary model and paradigm for gospel hospitality and draws on four characteristics found in this story: readiness, risk, repentance, and recognition.[23] Translating these qualities into her model of gospel hospitality she defines readiness as watchfulness, and an attitude of expectancy. She ties this readiness to early Christian tradition, applying both to hosts and to guests: "-ready to welcome, ready to enter another's world, ready to be vulnerable."[24]

The second feature of gospel hospitality is risk, which Oden describes as awareness of the risks of rejection, physical abuse, and change. As Oden maintains, welcoming "the stranger" is risky, and it changes everyone and everything. Things are not the same after such hospitality, either for the hosts or guests.[25] Connected to risk is repentance, defined by Oden not as an emotion or state of regret, but of changing one's mind or direction. This is best defined in her own words:

> You know that you have been changed by your encounters, and that's what repentance is all about. We approach the edge of the unfamiliar and cross it, if only by a step. When we are received into God's life and, in turn, receive others, we encounter something new, whether we are the host or the guest.[26]

The final characteristic, recognition, is reminiscent of Richard Spear's discussion of "noticing," but in this case it is more than seeing, it is seeing others as God sees us, looking beyond appearances to perceive who we really are.[27] As Oden observes, Jesus was often noted as seeing beyond appearances and encountering persons at the level of their deepest longing and authenticity.[28] Such a depth of recognition is one of the greatest gifts we can offer one another.

23. Ibid., 17.
24. Ibid., 18.
25. Oden., 20.
26. Ibid., 23.
27. Ibid.
28. Ibid, 25.

Context, content, and the practice of radical hospitality are essential elements of any healthy practical ministry with transgender and gender non-conforming persons, and they were guiding themes and continual considerations in creating the retreat described in this book. The context was the lives and collective experience of gender non-conforming and transgender persons, for whom this retreat was planned. The central content was spiritual autobiography, and the central approach was radical hospitality. Together, these three considerations affected every decision for the retreat from choosing space to creating a program through which participants could share spiritual stories and practices. In the next chapter, we explore the experience of the retreat itself.

5

The Retreat

The retreat which emerged from research, theological reflection, and conversations with others proved to be a vital approach to ministry with gender non-conforming and transgender persons. Months of planning and preparation followed input from the questionnaire and subsequent email conversations with participants, and culminated in an overnight retreat that took place in August of 2015. This chapter is a description of that retreat and describes four key essentials: participants, theme and setting, program, and evaluations. Each section builds upon the other, and the chapter is loosely chronological in order. While largely descriptive the chapter illustrates and points toward the conclusions that follow in the final chapter.

The only prerequisite for participating in the retreat was identifying as transgender or gender non-conforming. I was intentionally general about requirements because I hoped to have a diverse representation of ages, life experience, religious background, and gender expression among those who attended. I contacted academic institutions, particularly theological schools; advocacy and non-profit organizations serving the transgender community; and colleagues who focused on transgender and gender non-conforming persons in their professional work. Initial contact with potential participants was made through email and social media such as Facebook. Electronic communication remained the primary means of communication, except for a few telephone conversations for clarification. One person who was without email received mailed hardcopies of all the retreat materials and information.

A brief description of the final group of retreatants is helpful at this point. Limited to fourteen participants, I initially thought it may be difficult to find fourteen transgender persons willing to engage in the project. I was wrong. Within the first days of sending out an invitational flyer two persons had contacted me asking for more information. This number grew to eight within two months. Some of the early respondents also provided names of persons they thought may be interested, which broadened my range of invitation. By the beginning of June I had fourteen participants and two on a waiting list. One person registered for the retreat withdrew during the month of June, and one individual registered only a month prior to the event.

The final group consisted of fourteen transgender or gender non-conforming persons ranging from mid-twenties to mid-seventies in age. The median age was 52. Four persons identified as gender non-conforming; four identified as transgender women; five identified as transgender men; and one identified as intersex. Seven lived in Massachusetts; others came from further away, from places such as Oregon, Florida, Connecticut, Pennsylvania, and New York. Some had participated in other types of transgender events, but for three persons this was their first gathering with other gender non-conforming individuals. Some were leaders within the lgbtq population and others were living stealth. Interestingly, while the retreat was not limited to or advertised as Christian, all the retreatants came from such a background, and some were currently affiliated with a Christian-based faith community, including six who were either pastoral or lay leaders within their congregations.

Many participants shared a history of rejection by early faith communities when issues around gender identity arose. This was true whether the persons openly shared their gender identity or remained quiet about it but continually heard condemnatory messages regarding transgender persons from the pulpit, Sunday school, and/or members of their congregation. For example, one person raised in an assortment of independent, evangelical churches shared their gender identity to the congregation and was told they were demon possessed and needed to pray for healing.[1] In this case, healing meant conforming to the appearance and role of the gender assigned at birth. The consequence of this experience was alienation from

---

1. I will consciously diverge from standard practices of gender-based singular and plural pronouns to conform to the pronoun usage in transgender and gender non-conforming communities.

the church that lasted more than six years. Other people offered similar stories. Overall, virtually every participant bore the scars of religious abuse and mistreatment by either individual Christians, a church, or faith-based organizations or communities.

Given such a common history of negative church experience, some might expect reports of ongoing bitterness and spiritual isolation. While participants freely shared such experiences and clearly wanted to tell these stories, several also told positive stories of discovering other sources and places of spiritual community. At one time or another during group activities, every participant spoke of the importance of spiritual life and practices in their personal lives. Some present shared stories of how their faith helped them endure life prior to affirming their transgender, intersex or gender non-conforming identity. Many spoke of life as a spiritual journey on which transgender persons offer a unique perspective and fill a unique place. However, alongside this affirmation one lament shared by several present was a sense of isolation and loneliness even in the midst of welcoming congregations. People explained that an accepting community sometimes placed the burden of education and advocacy upon the transgender person(s), and then offered no support plans or practical ministries.

The theme and title of the retreat, "Spiritual Autobiography and Story as Sources of Spiritual Renewal" sounded self-explanatory to me, but input gleaned from the questionnaires and email conversations revealed different concepts of what that meant to others in terms of 1. What type of setting and ambience were desirable. 2. How stories were shared 3. What kinds of activities were engaged. The dynamic between "outside team" and "inside team" as described by Helen Cameron et al in *Talking about God in Practice* was helpful to me in understanding this process and utilizing it to create a positive retreat experience.[2] You can read in more detail about this methodology in the addendum. Briefly, in the method outlined in the text there are always two "teams" involved in a process. One team is composed of those seeking resources in understanding a particular issue or concern and moving toward a new paradigm. The other team is the "outsider team." These are the persons who serve as facilitators and resource the process. Recognizing my role as a member of the "outsider team" (facilitator) allowed me to gather important information, and listen with a different set of ears to the "insider team" (retreatants) before, during, and following the event. In classic theological action research a function of the outside team

2. See: Cameron et al, *Talking About God in Practice*, 64–65.

is to assist the organization or faith-based community in articulating differences between espoused and operating theology among the group.[3] In this case, there was no one, single operant theology among the retreatants, but the insights gleaned from the questionnaire and email conversations helped facilitate a retreat experience grounded in the articulated hopes and needs expressed in these materials.

Setting and ambience were clearly significant considerations. In the early stages of planning, I deliberated over five different retreat settings. The first was a local retreat center operated by the Roman Catholic Church, but it was obvious this would be an obstacle to some participants. Three members of our group spoke of being verbally abused by priests or nuns serving in the local parish; one shared a story of disclosing their gender identity in confession only to be told to leave and not return until repenting of this sin. Because of various articles written by the Roman Catholic Church concerning gender identity I also did not know if our group would be welcome and so I did not pursue this option.

The second possible choice was a Buddhist meditation center near Boston. Because everyone in the group identified as Christian in some form and practice, this also did not seem like the best selection. As with the Roman Catholic center I did not know if our group would be welcome here either, but, once again, other obstacles such as accessibility and location rendered that a moot point. A third option and the one toward which I was first drawn was Rolling Ridge Retreat Center, which is owned and operated by The United Methodist Church. While the denomination currently espouses unsupportive policies and practices concerning lgbtq persons, there are those within the denomination supporting full inclusivity and I knew this center was a safe and welcoming environment. I did have reservations, however; one of which was the distance of the Rolling Ridge Camp and Retreat Center from Boston and the lack of public transportation.

I already had made a preliminary contact with Rolling Ridge Retreat Center when the first round of email conversations revealed that such a setting was not appealing to several potential participants. Participant comments indicated essential concerns regarding agency or the capacity to exert power within the situation and setting. For some people this meant that a retreat center located in a remote setting was far too isolated. One person said they would feel trapped in such an environment, particularly without an automobile. Another individual expressed the importance of

3. Cameron et al., 104–105.

knowing they could leave at any time if necessary and felt being in an unfamiliar, isolated location would make this more difficult. Two persons who travelled by plane to the retreat also indicated it would be very difficult to arrange transportation to and from the airport. Many also desired a more urban location, one in which it was possible to walk to coffee or other stores during break times.

After taking all feedback into consideration one option remained: The Walker Center-Ecumenical Exchange, located in Newton, Massachusetts. This center also has a long history associated with The United Methodist Church and like Rolling Ridge has a policy of welcome and inclusivity. Unlike Rolling Ridge, The Walker Center is central to the city and easily accessible by public transportation. It is close to many coffee shops and small eateries. An additional positive attribute is its multi-functional use as a retreat center, a center for ecumenical and inter-faith gatherings, and a bed and breakfast. Because three retreatants flew or drove from great distances it was important that people had a place they could either reserve a day or two in advance, or arrange to stay late, after the retreat was over. This was especially helpful for one member of our group who planned a longer stay in Boston than the others.

Tracy, a member of The Walker Center staff with whom I had worked on previous occasions was our main contact person for this retreat, and I felt very comfortable working with her on the logistics as well as needs of this retreat. A contract was arranged that suited our needs: we would be centered in a small house on the grounds that comfortably held fifteen, the exact number of our group. We would share meals with one other group, an annual international meeting of youth from Israel, Pakistan, and the United States seeking to foster understanding among different religions and cultures. This sounded like the type of organization with which we could share space, so I proceeded to arrange the retreat in this setting.

It had been two years since my last visit to The Walker Center and I wanted to meet the co-directors as well as other staff, so I arranged to visit the space again prior to the retreat. I also wanted to walk through the house in which we would stay so I could better plan rooms and roommates, snacks, and some of the retreat activities that would take place in the house. The visit went exceptionally well, and the staff helped arrange everything we needed for our stay including special dietary needs and use of projection equipment. I left that visit feeling our group would be safe and welcome.

When we did finally gather in August the sense of authentic welcome and hospitality exuded by all the staff put everyone at ease. When the retreat ended, new friendships had been formed between Walker Center staff and some participants. In the spirit of Margaret Guenther's "welcoming the stranger"[4] and Amy Oden's "gospel hospitality"[5] we were provided with safety, all we needed for survival, and genuine human companioning by the staff with whom we shared space. Risks were taken by all, surprises were discovered, and, as gospel hospitality affirms, everyone was changed.

The retreat program was also created with input provided by the participants. For example, no one desired to begin the retreat early on Saturday so we planned for a "soft start" that morning; allowing a full hour between arrival and first gathering. As it turned out the beginning was even softer than this, as one person was already at the Walker Center following an earlier conference and moved into the house with us on Friday night. Another participant arrived Friday evening on a flight from Florida and met us at the house that night as well. The remaining retreatants arrived Saturday morning from as early in the morning as six o'clock until almost ten, the time when we first met as a group.

Feedback from the questionnaire also indicated this group preferred a lot of interaction, so the schedule and activities were all planned with this in mind. Gift bags that included small journals and a pen were given as people arrived to encourage personal writing and reflection during the retreat. These bags were designed to help put people at ease and included snacks and fun items such as bubbles. To begin our focus on story we engaged in an ice-breaker activity known as Activity Protocol, designed to allow the exploration and sharing of stories on a safe level. As each person arrived and registered they were given a pad of colorful sticky notes and invited to write brief, one or two word descriptive personal characteristics. For example, one of the words I included was "husband." People then posted these on a large blank wall in our main meeting room. This wall had been "seeded" earlier with examples from myself and a few others. When everyone was finished, we had quite a colorful wall with many groupings of life experiences and personal characteristics. Sitting in a large circle we each responded to three rounds of prompts/questions about what we had posted: 1. What is one identity you definitely want people in this group to know? 2. What is one identity that most people do not know about you and

4. Guenther, Holy Listening, 9–10.
5. Oden, 11.

are surprised to learn? 3. What is one identity that was once important to you but not so much anymore? These prompts, intentionally open-ended, helped begin conversation and the sharing of personal stories at a level with which each person was comfortable.

As we gathered in our first circle we shared names, preferred pronouns and other general information. It was during this time that I shared how my interest in creating this retreat developed. I spoke of my personal experience of God as transgender and how that developed through religious studies and spiritual practices. Many others present shared from their own experience. I also spoke briefly about how authentic expression of my religious experience necessitates terms that express God in transgender language as well. I concluded this time by introducing the group to Julian of Norwich, a thirteenth century Christian mystic who wrote of her experience of God in gender-fluid language. I shared short excerpts from her *Showings*[6] and placed this and other resource books on a table for use during the remainder of our time together. We also created our group covenant. These were the ground rules by which we would live and share life together for the next twenty-six hours:

- Use "I" statements
- Speak to the group
- Respect the opinion of others
- Be mindful of time
- Step up/ step back
- Project-speak up
- Everyone participate
- Self-care
- Confidentiality
- No photos during program or without consent

These were listed on newsprint and displayed in our conference room throughout the retreat. Before the first break we engaged in one more ice-breaker, interactive activity, "Continuum Dialogue." This was a simple

6. For this retreat, I drew from chapters 59, 60, and 86. Chapters 59 and 60 speak of the Motherhood of God and Christ; chapter 86 concludes the book, revealing that the ultimate purpose of everything God has created is love, and that love will reconcile all things in the end.

exercise in which people moved to various places in the room depending on preferred responses to questions such as, "Would you rather live in the mountains or at the beach?" This was an easy activity that involved movement and a variety of groupings as people responded. Some of the questions also included things related to gender identity or gender roles.

Even though this group desired more time for interaction than introspection, it seemed important to provide adequate time and space for breaks, personal writing and reflection. The initial break was brief, only ten minutes, but it provided some space after these introductory and sharing activities. When we regrouped, our next activity was a writing exercise that also became the first opportunity for sharing in pairs. As in the earlier activities, participants were invited to only share things with which they were comfortable. The exercise was simple: write a story about your hair, a meal, or an animal. These prompts were also open-ended, allowing for sharing personal stories at a variety of levels. We shared our stories in pairs at first, then in the larger group as time allowed. This activity took us to lunch, our first meal together, and with the staff and international youth group.

The Dining Room experience was a blend of gracious hospitality offered by the staff, diverse cultures among and within the two groups, and youthful curiosity and energy. I had met the adult leaders of the youth and knew they had talked openly with them about our group, and being respectful. This resulted in a positive experience, although the noise level in the room during meals sometimes made conversation among our group impossible. In addition, the curiosity of some members of the youth gathering was obvious in long stares at our group. Although no one mentioned this, I wondered if the stares impacted anyone. Overall, it was a constructive experience, although in the future this may be a factor in selecting a site for additional retreats. It would be optimal to have private space and a quieter atmosphere to facilitate conversation. Fortunately, the tables we sat at were round, and this helped the ability of small groups to talk together during meals.

The longest break followed lunch. This was also intentional. More than one retreatant had expressed a need for a short nap during the day. Others wanted time for personal space. There was plenty of room for walking, and shops nearby for anyone who wanted time alone outdoors. I noticed one small group gathered on the lawn together and spent the break time in deep conversation. My first inclination was to join them. As I thought about this, I hesitated; I felt that my role as part of the "outside team" included facilitating conversation among the "insider team." This long break appeared like an excellent opportunity for "inside team" conversation, so I did not join that particular group.

When we reconvened the whole group engaged in an activity we called, "Theater Game." This was simple and open to endless possibilities. The game is also mostly non-verbal and it gave participants an opportunity to express story through body language. Initially two volunteers struck a pose after receiving a prompt. For example, "two people meeting" or "trust." With the next prompt, when someone in the circle was inspired, they went up and replaced one of the pair, including the other in the new interpretive pose. This was a very creative and improvisational type of activity. Everyone participated and appeared to enjoy it. After several rounds, the group debriefed the experience together and then moved back into our circle for the next activity, sharing object stories.

Among the items retreatants were asked to bring to the retreat and this session was a small object that held some particular meaning for them. Originally, I had planned for this piece to take place during our initial round of introductions. Feedback from other participants indicated that this kind of sharing would flow better following a sequence of less personal activities. With this in mind, the sharing of objects was moved in the schedule to Saturday afternoon. Originally planned for half an hour, this time of personal sharing demanded more time than allotted. It was one of those moments that Helen Cameron et al describe as Kairos time: "the right moment, the unplanned insight, the conversation that takes off when participants 'lose track of time.'"[7] It was clear from the depth of sharing that this was a very important moment for many of those present. After we shared our stories around these objects, we placed them on a windowsill altar space for the remainder of the retreat.

By this time, it was after three o'clock on Saturday afternoon. The group had experienced many activities together, and shared personal stories through a variety of formal and informal means. A few persons looked tired, while others seemed to have energy that continued to build. My ad hoc interpretation was that introverts and extroverts were responding differently, and that some were feeling the stress of being with a new group of people for such a concentrated time. One participant in particular mentioned needing quiet time. We took a short break after which we regrouped for an activity that turned out to be quite informative, moving and fun.

7. Cameron et al, 66.

In the next activity, each person was to select a favorite song. They were to choose a song that represented them in some way, and then, to be prepared to share the song and their reason for selecting it with the group. The leader of this activity created a playlist, and had a cellphone and a wireless speaker. We formed again into our large group and played the first song. After listening to the song, the person who chose it shared why it was important. The range of music was truly amazing, as were the stories that accompanied each chosen piece. For many, the story around the song revealed a time of deep personal struggle, determination, joy, or all the above having to do with faith, authenticity, and gender identity. This was a favorite activity, and the playlist so popular that I created a master list and sent it to each person following the retreat.

The one activity of the retreat that involved an outside guest and facilitator followed this songfest. Called simply "Prayer weaving," this was a writing and art activity that I had experienced in another setting. Because it did involve inviting a cis-gender person into our space, the group had been asked if this were an issue, and if they were open to the activity. The initial round of responses indicated everyone was open to this activity and facilitator, and so we did include it in the schedule. One participant who did not see the email for some time did respond and thought it best not to include this outside facilitator, but arrangements were already in place and it seemed the majority had responded affirmatively.

Prayer weaving is a personal, quiet and reflective time, which includes both writing and art components. For our group the theme was "Membering, Dismembering, & Re-Membering." We were asked to think about a particularly challenging time in life. After writing in response to a series of prompts given by our facilitator, we spent time in silence re-reading our words and thinking about the words, concepts, directions, and theology of what we had written. We were asked if writing any of it was difficult; and if it resonated as authentic to us now? The room was quiet for several minutes except for the sound of writing. Some wrote very long compositions, others did not fully fill the paper. I noticed one person rubbed their head several times throughout the prayer weaving.

In the next step, each person chose two sheets of pre-painted paper, and color markers. When everyone was seated again, we were asked to look at our materials and think of why we chose those particular colors of paper and pens. We were then asked other questions that related our color choices to other choices we had made in life. The next action followed this reflection as we transferred our words onto both sides of the sheets of painted paper, using whatever style and colors we desired. Once again, we reflected upon questions spoken by our facilitator. This time we thought about what words stood out, and why; what is changing and what remains constant in the story we created; and any other significant things related to our story/prayer picture at this point.

Dismembering was the next step in the prayer-weaving process, and more than one person expressed this as difficult, because it meant cutting the paper sheets and our writing into pieces-strips called "weavers." We were invited to pay attention to how it felt, cutting our story/prayer into fragments. We quietly reflected on what such shredding meant to us; if it might signify an area of life irreparably altered in some way?

The final part of this activity (other than de-briefing) appeared to be the most energetic and most social: Re-Membering. This was the time for actually weaving the strips of paper together, forming a new creation. The facilitator invited us to play with the weaving, deciding what shape and style we wanted, and how we wanted to piece things back together. We also thought about the original story/prayer created earlier and the ways it was transformed. We were asked to reflect on other times in life when member-ing, dismembering, and re-membering occur or have occurred. This led the group to a time of sharing and debriefing during which many shared their stories and the process of creating their weaving in detail.[8]

When the prayer weaving ended, we had a small break until dinner together at six p.m. in the Dining Room. It was a very full day, and Saturday evening was designed to be relaxing and fun. We met together in the Living Room of our retreat house for the closing event of the evening. It was a little small, but it felt good to be in the house and an informal environment. It was also right next to the kitchen, and we had plenty of snacks available.

The event was called "U-tube Film Festival." As with the songfest, in pre-retreat emails participants had been asked to select a short video, eight minutes or less, to share with the group. The clip could be something funny, inspiring, educational, or thought provoking. Although we endured a few technological glitches in the beginning, through the combined efforts of those in the group with laptops and computer skills, we were able to enjoy a creative and meaningful evening. The diversity of clips selected to share

---

8. This prayer-weaving activity is designed by Holly C. Benzenhafer who also facil-itated this portion of the retreat. She graciously allowed me to include her instructional handout in the appendices.

was wonderful. The group shared both profound and humorous clips about gender-identity. Some shared videos relevant to their faith. Lively discussion followed each clip. At some point, I noted that we had again slipped into Kairos time. Time appeared to stand still and pass quickly simultaneously. We began showing clips at seven-thirty in the evening, and several people were still watching at nine-thirty when I went to rest and make a few planning adjustments to the next day's schedule.

While I had envisioned some type of formal Sunday morning gathering, feedback again indicated this group had other preferences. The Walker Center offered breakfast from seven-thirty until nine-thirty in the morning so we opted for a slow beginning to the day with "breakfast at your own pace." This turned out to be a good idea for more than one reason. When I awoke Sunday morning a few changes had taken place during the night. First, the person I noticed rubbing their head developed a migraine headache around eleven o'clock Saturday night. They contacted the person in the main office rather than me, and decided to drive home. A second participant found the length and shape of beds in the house challenging. This person left for the night, driving to a nearby hotel and rejoining the group early Sunday morning. A third participant discovered important medication had been left at home, not too far away, drove back to get it, then decided to sleep there, returning early in the morning as well. This person also suffered from chronic back pain and found the beds in our house too difficult to manage. These changes made a slow start Sunday morning the best possible choice.

The changes overnight were not the only ones that affected Sunday morning and the remainder of the retreat. The original schedule planned an off-site event at a local nearby park. As the group discussed this however, there was not a lot of enthusiasm. More than one person questioned utilizing the time left together in cars traveling to and from the park. The weather was overcast as well. Another factor was the ability of some participants to navigate the type of terrain we might encounter. Finally, not everyone present was able to remain through lunch. With these considerations in mind, we created another plan for Sunday morning.

Following breakfast on Sunday, we gathered for the last time in our main meeting room. The closing activity in this room was a writing exercise in which retreatants wrote a letter to themselves ten years in the future. The letter might offer advice, encouragement, inspiration, challenges; hopes—whatever came to mind and heart. Each person was also given an envelope which they self-addressed and returned to me sealed, with the letter inside. Before the group received these instructions, I spoke once again about how this retreat came into focus and the role of Christian mysticism, particularly Julian of Norwich, in helping to begin a theological conversation about gender-fluid language for God, the radical love of God, and life as spiritual journey among transgender and gender non-conforming persons. I asked three questions:

1. Might Julian of Norwich offer a positive theological framework and symbology for transgender Christians?

2. How might the practice of writing spiritual autobiography function as a resource in exploring spirituality for persons who identify as transgender or gender non-conforming?

3. What might a transgender autobiographical theology look like?

As part of the conversation I shared a dream I had years earlier; it was a very powerful dream in which I had visited myself in the house in which I grew up. I was about twelve years old in the dream, an age when my gender identity was beginning to cause increasing emotional pain. In the dream, I encouraged my younger self, and said that things would get better. It was similar enough to the letter we would write to our future selves to make a connection with the activity.

After this introduction, participants settled down to write. The time allotted for writing was thirty minutes, but once again, more time was required as people were drawn into the process. The sound of tears was audible from time to time in the quiet room. The only other sound was an occasional scribbling on the paper. When everyone had finished their letters, and had placed them in the self-addressed envelope, I collected them in a larger envelope for future mailing at an unknown date.

The final event in our meeting room was filling out evaluation forms. These forms were anonymous. Participants knew the evaluations were important both for weighing the value of the current retreat and for informing the design of future retreats for transgender and gender non-conforming persons. When participants completed the evaluations, they placed them in a box. This was the final activity in the meeting room. As people completed the evaluations and turned them in, they left for the house to begin cleaning-up the space, packing personal belongings, and preparing for our closing time together. When the last person completed the evaluation form and placed it in the box, I picked it up and walked back to the retreat house.

At the house, we gathered in the living room for our last activity. We sat in a circle on sofas, chairs, and the floor. I had brought decorative stationary, and each piece had the name of one participant written at the top. We passed the pages around the circle and each member of the group wrote an affirmation about that particular person. This took the remainder of our time before lunch. When everyone had finished and we all had an opportunity to read, reflect, and share whatever we wanted about the papers or retreat, we closed our time together and walked to lunch in the Dining Room.

Three months passed before I read the evaluations. This was intentional. In writing a descriptive account of the retreat experience, I did not want to be influenced by knowing what the participants had said immediately after the event was over. This chapter concludes however, with a review of the evaluations in order to understand the self-reported effects of the retreat on participants, and to assess the potentially positive effects of this type of retreat ministry with transgender and gender non-conforming persons.

Eleven participants completed the evaluation. One member of our group had left Saturday evening due to a migraine headache and did not complete the form. The form consisted of three parts: program, technical/ logistics matters, and post-retreat spiritual evaluation. Responses from participants concerning each part affirmed the value, significance, and possible future benefits of such a retreat ministry. In the first section concerning program, one question asked if retreatants would consider participating in similar retreats in the future. Without exception, every person said they would like further opportunities for this type of gathering.

Other responses to questions in the program area revealed the importance of community and companionship. One person specifically described feeling isolated and lonely in advocacy work; another wrote of the "wonderful companionship" experienced during the retreat. Most shared that meeting others with similar experiences was significant. As one person said, "The people made all the difference." Beyond this, several mentioned feeling validated, welcome, and free to explore their spirituality and gender identity in a new way. One of the most powerful and unexpected comments I read was related to a safe space for transgender persons of faith: "I got to meet up with non-religion-hating transgender people . . . it was safe, healing, and hope engendering." As the comment reveals, this person had only met other transgender persons who hated any form of organized religion.

One person summed up their experience in four positive words, "It relaxed my soul."

Another strength frequently named in the evaluations was the hospitality of the staff and leadership provided by the "outside team." Participants described the staff as gracious, warm, helpful, and "fantastic." I found the positive responses to the facilitation of the retreat significant because it indicated a successful process of building a dynamic relationship between the inside and outside teams as described by Helen Cameron et al.[9] Along with staff and facilitator hospitality, many commented positively on the physical setting of the retreat. Most felt it was a rustic setting within an urban environment and appreciated the grounds and convenience of transportation and access to stores such as coffee shops. I noticed that many participants spent break times outside, walking or sitting on the grounds. Many also expressed appreciation for the cost involved to offer the retreat without charge and found the experience both inexpensive and comfortable. For three persons attending the retreat would have been impossible if there were meal and lodging costs involved. Given the statistics concerning transgender persons and poverty, the ability to provide the retreat without cost is a significant factor for the development of future retreats.

Responses to what was the most inspiring and/or helpful part of the retreat revealed the importance of connecting, community, and interactive activities. I had expected many participants to value quiet time for reflection and personal writing. While one person specifically named that as the most valued time—to, "sit with myself and be real,"-the majority said that being with like-minded people and experiencing a sense of belonging with other spiritual beings was the most transformative aspect of the retreat.

The preference for community was further revealed through preferences regarding the retreat program. The interactive group activities were selected as the most helpful and inspiring. Two persons specifically named the Affinity Protocol icebreaker game with post-it notes as a favorite.[10] This was an activity designed to begin story sharing and community building at a safe level and its success was reflected in the overall response. Two additional events that were often cited were the sharing of personal objects and their stories in our large group, and the sharing of U-Tube music and films.

9. Cameron et al, 64–65.

10. Affinity Protocol is a group activity developed by National School Reform Faculty for professional learning communities. To learn more about this and other Protocols visit the National School Reform Faculty at www.nsrfharmony.org.

These latter also involved the sharing of personal story utilizing music and video clips as prompts.

As a member of the outside team I had a privileged perspective from which to observe the building of community and relationships. Observing people relax, discover one another and share stories of common life experience in a safe space was enough for me to rate the retreat a success. As many stated in their evaluations, opportunities for this type of supportive and transformative gathering are far too rare. Three respondents voiced a desire to prolong this unique time together, expressly stating the desire for a longer retreat. One participant summarized comments made by several, "This safe space and connection with folks will be transformative as I go forth." Such comments clearly disclose the value of this time together for those who participated, and the potential of such a ministry among faith-based communities seeking to create authentic spiritual hospitality and positive spiritual practices with the transgender/gender-queer population.

6

More Than the Sum of Parts

This final chapter revisits some theological foundations upon which my work is based. I referenced this briefly in the first chapter of this text, but now is the time to further explore connections between information gathered from the retreat; the value of future retreat ministry with transgender and gender non-conforming persons affirmed in this retreat; and the spiritual mandate of mercy and grace taught and modeled by Jesus. I examine the evaluations and follow-up interviews through a reflective process suggested in, *Talking about God in Practice: Theological Action Research and Practical Theology*, suggest future possibilities and theological guidelines for such a proactive and hospitality-oriented ministry, and conclude with a theological reflection grounded in passages from the gospel.

The evaluations and follow-up interviews provided very positive feedback for the future of reflection, a process that ideally leads to renewed theology and practice within organizations.[1] Applying this process to the retreat varied from the traditional model. The most obvious differences were the absence of a physical joint meeting prior to, and following the retreat to reflect as a group. In this case I was only able to collect written data voluntarily provided by participants, together with the post-retreat interviews. I would change this when possible in creating other retreats, and hope that it is possible for other groups engaging in such a ministry to do so as well. I am certain the initial formation of two teams, the "insider team" and "outsider team" would benefit from such face-to-face meetings.

While limited in the ability to create physical gatherings before and following the retreat, the reflection questions offered by Cameron et al.

---

1. Cameron et al, *Talking about God in Practice*, 102–106.

were helpful in the process of evaluating and processing this event. In addition to providing many examples groups may find helpful in planning a retreat such as the one described in this text, *Talking about God in Practice* offers a detailed guideline to help process the experience. As with creating a time and space for physical meetings before and following such a retreat; the questions provided may improve the evaluation and reflection process among communities. The guide is created to be just that, a guide, and some of the questions may not fit a particular situation. Other helpful questions may arise. Each retreat is a unique experience. These questions were helpful in assessing the gathered responses from my retreat.[2] Reframing the questions in the guide to fit this project and following the suggested process were invaluable tools for reflecting on and understanding the information provided by retreatants and my experience as a facilitator. I composed a list of the following questions and considered each one as I read through the evaluations and interview responses:

1. Does the data help answer the research question?

2. Is there anything surprising about the data?

3. What are the implicit values and beliefs embedded in the data?

4. Is there anything that affirms the beliefs and values of this project?

5. Is there anything that challenges the beliefs and values of this project?

6. Where do you see God in the data?

7. What did I learn and what actions would I suggest in moving forward?

The answers to these questions will guide the remainder of this section of the chapter.

All the data gathered from the participants indicated that retreat ministries in general, and storytelling and spiritual autobiography in particular, facilitated spiritual renewal. For example, the evaluation form asked participants if they would be inclined to attend another retreat, or to recommend this type of retreat to someone else. Of those completing the interview, all replied in the affirmative. One person responded "possibly." The most affirming comment related to this project was the response of one person when asked if they had anything else to add, "Just a Thank you for doing this work. It would be a beautiful thing for all the transgender community to have this kind of retreat." This simple and moving summary is a powerful

---

2. Cameron et al, 178.

indicator of what such a ministry may offer many in the transgender and gender non-conforming community.

Several things surprised me about the data, and the retreat experience itself. While the pre-retreat survey and emails indicated this group preferred community-building and networking activities, I was still surprised by how quickly the group bonded, and by the spiritual depth that emerged in such a short period of time. In such a diverse group, the meaning of spiritual varied. One person expressed this as awareness of the presence of Christ. Another retreatant connected with the Two Spirit energy of the group. The spiritual core uniting the group resulted in diverse expressions of a collective human journey seeking and sharing stories of ultimate meaning.[3] Such expressions point toward the power of story in spiritual companionship and formation.

From the beginning, there was an atmosphere of genuineness and realism that drew the group together and facilitated deep personal sharing. One person described the retreat as a wonderful spiritual bonding experience. Another said, "I think it was important that religious practice, values, and belief were guiding the group process, but not taught to the group." Others commented about the camaraderie within the entire group, and one person added that this is what made every activity meaningful.

Another unanticipated positive benefit of the retreat was the setting. While I knew ease of access and sense of safety were important concerns for everyone in the group, I had underestimated the importance of setting in terms of the presence of a welcoming staff, green space within an urban area, and a safe space in which to relax enough to build community and relieve isolation. One participant specifically noted the importance of our informal time together-meals and breaks, and the opportunity to connect casually with everyone, including staff members: "I think fellowship is very important for breaking down isolation and lessening loneliness—-and I have been isolated and lonely/longing for safe space to exhale." Once again, the simple profundity of this statement affirms the potential power of a retreat ministry with and for those who identify as transgender and gender non-conforming.

One additional surprise in the retreat was the willingness and desire of several members of our group to participate in leadership. All communication prior to our gathering included invitations to suggest and/or lead activities, and while participants had offered suggestions about setting and

3. Frankl, *Man's Search for Ultimate Meaning*, 28.

content, only one person expressed an interest in leading an activity. When we actually gathered, however, and as people became more comfortable, they moved naturally into roles of shared leadership and responsibility. For example, as people arrived, those who had come early offered help to new arrivals in finding their rooms, receiving nametags, and locating the meeting and dining rooms in the main building. Others helped prepare snacks in the kitchen located in our retreat house. The house soon filled with the sounds of a community enjoying food and conversation in a relaxed atmosphere.

An activity Saturday evening provided several members of the group an opportunity to share leadership. We had planned a U-Tube video fest and invited each person to select a segment eight minutes or less to share that night. We created a playlist. Several technical problems arose, however, including problems with a projector and computer needed for the program. Fortunately, one person had a computer that could connect to everything correctly, and others knew how to help connect it to the U-tube site. Although this process took several minutes, the community effort deepened the connections among the group and people visibly relaxed. The video fest actually extended well past the scheduled time as persons chose additional videos to share and discuss together.

As an observer and facilitator of the retreat, I noticed common values and beliefs operating within the community even before I read the evaluations. The three most obvious were, the transgender nature of God, the diversity of the divine Spirit, and the resultant ethical command to honor and respect diverse expressions of human life. Several members commented on their experience of God as transgender, although that term varied in meaning among retreatants. Some imaged God as beyond gender. For example, one retreatant refrained from language that might imply any gendered or anthropomorphic God remarking, "I tend to connect more seriously with God than closely with other human beings. I enjoy a congregation, but I connect first with The Source and trust only in The Source." Another participant shared their experience of visioning the Holy Spirit as a feminine expression of God. Others shared a vision of God as pure light or energy, and Jesus as the human form of this energy. Only one had heard of Julian of Norwich, but several expressed deep interest in her experience and expression of God as it resonated with their own use of non-binary language and imagery.

One member of our group commented about transgender spirituality: "In my Native American community we are honored and revered because we are closer to the Great Spirit. The Great Spirit is both male and female and so are we." This comment and others led to a conversation about diverse expressions of the Spirit. For some this meant the Holy Spirit within the Christian tradition, but several traditions in addition to Christianity were mentioned as contributing insights into the relationship between God and human gender identity. People named Judaism, Tibetan Buddhism, and Wicca as three examples of religions whose traditions include theological conversations specifically related to transgender persons.[4] A common thread in this discussion was the transgender nature and diverse expression of the Divine Spirit (Christian or otherwise) as it differed from conventional social concepts of gender. This was another connecting point for some with Julian of Norwich as well.

The group covenant we created early in the retreat illustrated the importance of mutual respect and care for one another. This value was apparent in how the group formed from the beginning. In the evaluations, one person described how the identities of being transgender and spiritual meld together, leading to a desire to see God in each person: "My spirituality is who I am, as is my transgender experience. The language of selfhood I've developed comes from both communities and those identities are inseparable." These implicit values: the transgender nature of God, the diversity of the Spirit, and respect for diverse expressions of life and faith were communicated through interactions among retreatants, the staff, and the other group with whom we shared space on occasion.

The data gathered before and after the retreat, combined with observations of the retreat itself, affirms the proposal that a retreat ministry may provide spiritual renewal, resources and practices for those who identify and transgender or gender non-conforming. All data and conversation related to this project revealed a deep sense of spirituality among the participants. While specific practices and traditions varied, every participant spoke or wrote about the spiritual core of their lives. Several described how they were led by this sense of spiritual connection to seek supportive communities, relationships, and practices.

Though many had faced rejection by at least one congregation, and others had not yet located a safe community, they articulated a strong sense

---

4. Williams, "Buddhist Bigots, Buddhism, and Trans Folk," August 3, 2013. http://www.transadvocate.com/buddhist-bigots-buddhism-and-trans-folk_n_9904.

of connection between being transgender and spirituality. Several spoke of their longing for a place to explore and practice spiritual expression within community. The retreat, while brief, provided a doorway to such community. It also extended the horizon of future possibilities, including the unspoken yet present potential of creating enduring connections between transgender and gender non-conforming persons, and safe, welcoming communities of faith.

Two unanticipated challenges arose that affected group dynamics. The first is individual personality characteristics. I had assumed a relative similarity among retreat participants in terms of planning large and small group activities, personal breaks, and quiet reflection time. As in any group, ours was a mix of introverts and extroverts. At times I observed the pace and duration of interaction appeared taxing for some participants. We tried to address this in our group covenant by encouraging people to use self-care. Still, the schedule and amount of large group activity seemed taxing for two of the quietest participants. Conversely, maintaining the interest and enthusiasm of more extroverted participants required such interaction. Facilitating the retreat to help draw introverts out, while preserving the enthusiasm and energy of the extroverts was a related concern.

A second challenge was trying to create a balance between spiritual expression and formal religion. The evaluations indicated that all of the participants were raised in the Christian tradition. Those traditions varied in form however, from Roman Catholic and Episcopalian, to Unitarian Universalist, and a self-created amalgamation of Christian and Native American Two-Spirit traditions. The difficulty in meeting the needs of all the participants for formal worship time was most clearly expressed by the comments of two participants, both from more orthodox Christian traditions, who missed a formal religious service as part of the retreat. Another person stated they thought there would be more study related to Scripture but did not say if they had desired more or not. On the other hand, some commented on their appreciation of the absence of any particular religious tradition or form of worship.

Discerning where God is present in the data (the sixth question in Appendix II: Guide to Reading Data[5]) is more difficult to answer, partly because it is subjective. The remark of one participant summarizes well how people viewed and honored one another as what many described as a common journey: "Sharing with others the various ways each of us have

5. Cameron et al, 178.

relationships with one Spirit, faith, or belief helped reconnect to my roots and remember what I valued in my faith community previously." Several participants wrote or spoke about the connection between their experience as transgender and spiritual. Some named struggles to discern between genuine faith and belief in the midst of a community or family using theology to justify rejection and abandonment. Many shared stories of the Spirit as a source of hope and strength in all times and circumstances. Clearly, God was present through the information shared in the data, particularly the questionnaire and evaluations, and throughout the retreat as people shared stories about their personal spiritual journey. One retreatant remarked about this saying, "In many ways I came into this weekend without expectations and uncertain about what or where there would be opportunities for spiritual growth. Hearing various experiences provided a broader foundation for working across varied faith communities." The participants were able to see and experience the presence of God through the shared activities and conversations provided by the retreat.

The greatest learning that I take away from this project is the potential of this type of retreat ministry for spiritual renewal among the transgender and gender non-conforming population, and for those who sponsor and staff these retreats. Along with the many affirmations expressing hopes of finding a safe spiritual home came hurtful memories of past rejection, or the present and difficult search for a safe and genuinely welcoming faith community. One person spoke and wrote about how hard it is to find a place to belong, and the strength it takes to keep walking through new doors into a sea of strangers hoping that this may be the place. Many nodded in agreement. The issue of trust was central in these stories. As I listened and reflected on what was shared it was clear that a retreat ministry can begin building a bridge of trust.

As I discuss in the Addendum, participatory action research is uniquely suited for ministry with transgender and gender non-conforming people. The interactive foundation of this model provides agency and voice to and among a disempowered and marginalized population. The insider and outsider teams created in the theological action research model generated by Cameron, Bhatti, et. al[6] creates an equalization of power and voice among facilitators and participants that is essential for providing a safe, welcoming, and empowering space.

6. Cameron et al.

The organic process of theological action research is also an unexpected benefit for creating future retreats. Because participants are also co-creators, every retreat is unique, and the direct result of the dynamic interaction among everyone involved. This may be valuable especially in working with persons who are members of racial, ethnic, or other minority groups even further marginalized than the transgender and gender nonconforming community in general.

For example, results from the most recent national transgender survey revealed the following:

- Discrimination was pervasive for all respondents who took the National Transgender Discrimination Survey, yet the combination of anti-transgender bias and persistent, structural and individual racism was especially devastating for Black transgender people and other people of color.

- Black transgender people live in extreme poverty with 34% reporting a household income of less than $10,000/year. This is more than twice the rate for transgender people of all races (15%), four times the general Black population rate (9%), and over eight times the general US population rate (4%).

- Black transgender people are affected by HIV in devastating numbers. Over one-fifth of Black respondents were HIV-positive (20.23%) and an additional 10% reported that they did not know their status. This compares to rates of 2.64% for transgender respondents of all races, 2.4% for the general Black population, and 0.60% of the general US population.

- Nearly half (49%) of Black respondents reported having attempted suicide.

- Black transgender people who were out to their families found acceptance at a higher rate than the overall sample of transgender respondents.[7] This was significant in terms of positive outcome

In addition to these statistics, the newly released 2015 National Transgender Discrimination Survey provides concrete data illustrating that when ethnicity and race are examined among respondents a troubling pattern emerges. Poverty, unemployment, healthcare, people living with HIV,

---

7. National Black Justice Coalition, "Injustice at Every Turn" http://nbjc.org/sites/default/files/trans-adjustment-web.pdf.

homelessness, and violence are all intensified among non-white transgender respondents. For example, among all respondents 1.4% lived with HIV (five times the national rate), among Black participants the rate increased to 6.7%. This is significantly higher. The rate among Black transgender women was an overwhelming 19%.[8] Respondents with disabilities also reported facing higher degrees of mistreatment, unemployment, poverty, and an increased risk of suicide.[9] Another sobering fact is that among the names read each year during Transgender Day of Remembrance observances the majority are transgender women of color. This includes statistics from the United States.[10] The brutal deaths of Shante Thompson and her companion Willie Sims are two tragic examples recorded in 2016.[11] Such statistics underscore the need for positive and proactive ministries with transgender persons of color.

A ministry grounded in agency, solidarity, and mutuality is invaluable for ministry among the most vulnerable among the transgender and gender non-conforming community. A retreat model offers such a ministry as participants create a retreat that reflects the cultural, racial, and theological diversity, preferences, and issues unique to that group.

The interactive and participatory focus of the participatory action method engaged in this event allowed every person to have a voice in the creation and implementation of the retreat. This participation and agency helped to build trust before the actual event, helped establish a sense of belonging and ownership during the retreat, and contributed to the atmosphere of welcome shared among retreatants, facilitators, and staff. Trust was built before the actual event as the facilitators responded to the expressed needs and hopes of potential participants through the questionnaire, and emails while creating the retreat. That this process helped establish a sense of belonging and ownership during the retreat was obvious in the way participants naturally took on welcoming and leadership roles. One result of this shared sense of ownership was the degree of hospitality and welcome shared among the participants.

The written and spoken information gathered in this retreat process confirm that such a retreat ministry created with and for persons who

---

8. The Center for Transgender Equality, "2015 National Transgender Discrimination Survey," 6.

9. Ibid., 7

10. The Task Force, "Stop Trans Murders."

11. Good, "Transgender Woman among Two Killed in Late-Night Houston Shooting."

identify as transgender or gender non-conforming is a powerful means of spiritual renewal. The emphasis on sharing story and spiritual autobiography through a variety of activities, media, and conversations also affirmed the importance, possibility and power of such retreats to give voice to marginalized persons, a voice that needs to be heard by the speaker, the group, and the larger community.[12] The remainder of this chapter explores why such a retreat ministry is important for the health and well-being, not only of those who identify as transgender and gender non-conforming, but also of those who identify as cis-gendered persons of faith. Within this section, the focus is specifically on those who identify as followers of Jesus.

Returning to the theological basis of this text; the Christian life is one committed to following the example and teaching of Jesus. Regardless of theological differences or preferred translation of the Bible, one essential mandate preceding all others is love of God and neighbor. Such love and hospitality goes far beyond the traditional cultural boundaries of hospitality both then, and today. Jesus invites us further, into life that is willing to risk surprises, change, and transformation. This instruction is reinforced several places in the gospels but the story told by Jesus that explicitly underscores this is The Parable of the Good Samaritan examined in chapter 1. Above everything else, this is a story of radical love and hospitality that precedes religious tradition or dogma. It is a story worthy of reading, and after everything you have read up to this point I invite you to read it again:

> Just then a lawyer stood up to test Jesus. "Teacher," he said, "what must I do to inherit eternal life?" He said to him, "What is written in the law? What do you read there?" He answered, "You shall love the Lord your God with all your heart, and with all your soul, and with all your strength, and with all your mind; and your neighbor as yourself." And he said to him, "You have given the right answer; do this, and you will live."
>
> But wanting to justify himself, he asked Jesus, "And who is my neighbor?" Jesus replied, "A man was going down from Jerusalem to Jericho, and fell into the hands of robbers, who stripped him, beat him, and went away, leaving him half dead. Now by chance a priest was going down that road; and when he saw him, he passed by on the other side. So likewise, a Levite, when he came to the place and saw him, passed by on the other side. But a Samaritan while traveling came near him; and when he saw him, he was moved with pity. He went to him and bandaged his wounds, having

12. Phan and Jung Young Lee, eds., *Journeys at the Margins.*

poured oil and wine on them. Then he put him on his own animal, brought him to an inn, and took care of him. The next day he took out two denarii, gave them to the innkeeper, and said, 'Take care of him; and when I come back, I will repay you whatever more you spend.' Which of these three, do you think, was a neighbor to the man who fell into the hands of the robbers?" He said, "The one who showed him mercy." Jesus said to him, "Go and do likewise."

This core story and teaching of Jesus relate directly to the work of a retreat ministry with transgender persons.

Like Samaritans and the dead in the time of Jesus, transgender and gender non-conforming persons today are one of the most marginalized populations on earth. This has been illustrated repeatedly by surveys such as "*Injustice at Every Turn*" and the rising numbers of deaths reported each year during Transgender Day of Remembrance observances.[13] Despite such a clear example in the teaching of Jesus concerning right relationship between God and neighbor, many denominations and local congregations continue to either ignore or vilify the existence of this entire community. They are like those in Jesus' parable who, driven by fear of contamination and social rejection themselves, evade contact with the wounded victim, even crossing the road to avoid being proximate to one viewed as unclean.

Avoiding societal rejection by association is not a fear limited to the first century. A recent poll by the Pew Research Center revealed the broad spectrum of policies concerning transgender members in various denominations.[14] According to this data, although religious bodies are now addressing the participation of transgender persons in their congregations in a formal way, there is much controversy and debate over the authenticity, religious value, and acceptance of this community. The Episcopal, Unitarian Universalist and United Church of Christ all have an official statement of inclusion concerning transgender persons. The Union for Reform Judaism recently passed a resolution affirming a commitment to full inclusivity and acceptance of people expressing a variety of gender identities.[15]

---

13. Grant, et al, "The National Transgender Discrimination Survey: Full Report."

14. Sandstrom, "Religious Groups' Policies on Transgender Members Vary Widely," December 2, 2015, http://www.pewresearch.org/fact-tank/2015/12/02/religious-groups-policies-on-transgender-members-vary-widely/.

15. Unitarian Universalist Association, "Lesbian, Gay, Bisexual, Transgender, and Queer Justice"; United Church of Christ, "L,G,B,T Ministries"; The Episcopal Church, "L,G,B,T in the Church"; Union for Reform Judaism, "Resolution on the Rights of Transgender and Gender Non-Conforming People."

Other faith communities and denominations such as the Southern Baptist Convention, Assemblies of God and Lutheran Church Missouri Synod outright bar transgender and gender non-conforming people from participation in their congregations. The Southern Baptist Convention passed a resolution in 2014 proclaiming that transgender persons can only become members if they agree to repent.[16] The Roman Catholic Church does not even recognize transgender persons, stating that gender is determined permanently by the estimation of others at ones birth.[17] The pope recently compared the recognition of gender identity theory and recognition of transgender persons with the destructive capacity of nuclear weapons in terms of each ones capacity to cause human and natural destruction: "Let's think of the nuclear arms, of the possibility to annihilate in a few instants a very high number of human beings," Pope Francis says. "Let's think also of genetic manipulation, of the manipulation of life, or of the gender theory, that does not recognize the order of creation."[18] While this language does not specifically point out transgender persons this statement combined with others only adds to the justification of social and political oppression and violence directed towards this population of human beings.

Gender theory establishes distinctions between perceived biological sex and gender identity. It also considers socialization in understanding gender and gender behavior. Psychologists and feminists appropriated the term 'gender' in the 1960's to differentiate between biological sex and gender. Psychologists writing on transsexuality were the first to use gender terminology in this sense. To explain why some people felt that they were 'trapped in the wrong bodies,' the psychologist Robert Stoller (1968) began using the terms 'sex' to pick out biological traits and 'gender' to pick out the amount of femininity and masculinity a person demonstrated.[19] In refusing to acknowledge gender theory and distinctions between perceived biological sex and gender, Pope Francis, among other religious leaders, implicitly encourages the oppression of transgender and gender non-conforming persons.

Denominations such as the Presbyterian Church (U.S.A.) and The United Methodist Church currently have no official policy regarding

16. The Southern Baptist Convention, "On Transgender Identity."

17. Ibid., 3.

18. Saul, "Pope Francis Compares Arguments for Transgender Rights to Nuclear Arms Race."

19. Mikkola, "Feminist Perspectives on Sex and Gender."

transgender persons, but send mixed messages, and full participation or leadership by "out" transgender persons is either absent or negligible. This lack of official policy actually increases the difficulty of locating a safe faith community for gender non-conforming people because the local policies and behavior varies among congregations. I have had several conversations with transgender persons who mistakenly thought a nearby local church was safe because they had previously attended a welcoming, reconciling or otherwise inclusive church in another location. When they discover that the church is not welcoming to them this can be a traumatic experience.

The social and spiritual isolation resulting from societal marginalization and religious persecution leaves many transgender people either literally or figuratively traumatized, beaten and in need of physical and spiritual care. The story of Tina is one powerful example. I met Tina shortly after sharing my personal transgender story with the congregation I was serving. Members from local newspapers were also present, so the story quickly became public. Tina called my office one day a few weeks later to ask about an upcoming event at our church. We were hosting Peterson Toscano, at that time an activist for the lgbtq community who had written a play, "*Transfigurations: Transgressing Gender in the Bible.*" Tina wanted to attend the performance, and asked if she would be safe. Although she knew I am transgender, she still did not assume she would be welcome. I assured her she would be safe with us. Tina did attend the performance. Eventually Tina began attending church services and other events, and began an ongoing relationship of transformation for Tina and the congregations in which she participates.

When I met Tina the evening of Peterson's performance I knew little about her. Over time I learned Tina had not been to a church for any reason for several years. I also discovered that after facing rejection by some family members, friends, and members of the community in which she lived, Tina had moved into a small trailer in an old barn. This is where she lived for thirteen years, rarely going out except for groceries and other needs, and to earn money at part-time jobs. Most of Tina's leisure time, which often extended late into the night, was playing an online video game, "World of Warcraft." She stayed awake to play by eating tons of sugary snacks and drinking Mountain Dew. While she did keep in contact with a few friends and family members, she was isolated from a supportive pastor or faith community.

When I moved to another congregation the next year not far from the previous one, Tina moved, too. This congregation became a Reconciling Congregation, which in The United Methodist Church means a congregation that both welcomes and advocates for inclusivity with lgbtq people. With the support of this congregation Tina became very active in the life of the church. She regularly served as liturgist, helped serve Holy Communion, provided lots of elbow grease and physical labor, and contributed her ideas on several committees. In the two years during which I was pastor of that congregation Tina earned two perfect attendance pins for never missing a worship service. Tina truly cherished this award, as did the entire congregation.

Tina eventually moved from the area and found a new church home in her new place of residence. With the support of another Reconciling Congregation, Tina wears several leadership hats in her present faith community, and lovingly shares her many talents and gifts.

Tina's story is one of transformation; transformation not only for Tina but for all those who shared and continue to share life and ministry with her. This powerful and positive example of personal and congregational transformation resulted from the willingness of a group of strangers to embark upon a journey together, not really knowing where it would lead, or even what would be helpful, but trusting in the process of listening and discernment.

A retreat ministry is more concrete and intentionally defined than the initial seat-of-our-pants experience of those early years. Key components of the Good Samaritan story may be applied to a retreat ministry such as the one this text presents. These were also guiding principles for the retreat. The first and most obvious is the offer of this retreat at no cost to participants. The theological basis for offering a free retreat is taken directly from the parable of The Good Samaritan.

In the story Jesus tells, the man found robbed, beaten and left for dead by the roadside had no resources. He was left naked; with nothing. The Samaritan who stops to care for him cannot miss this apparent lack of resources. Nevertheless, the Samaritan lifts the injured man and takes him to the nearest inn. Once there, the Samaritan does not leave him at the door, or provide just enough money for an overnight stay. The Samaritan says the injured man is to receive care at the inn for however long is necessary and he will cover the bill. This begins the healing process. Similarly, offering a retreat at no cost and providing the essential necessities of safe space, food, shelter and companionship may begin or continue the healing process for participants.

A second detail sometimes overlooked in reading this parable is the provision of ongoing care and future relationship. This is neither a drop-off nor a one-time act of "paying it forward." The story communicates an implied potential for new and continuing relationships among the injured person, the Samaritan and the Innkeeper. The three represent the possibility of human solidarity and agency within a society bound by many religious traditions and laws. In the end Jesus asks, "Which one, do you think, was a neighbor to the man who fell into the hands of robbers?" When the lawyer responds by saying it was the one who showed mercy, Jesus simply says, "Go and do likewise." The profounder connection is the one between love of God and love of neighbor. If the Samaritan was the one who saw the beaten man as his neighbor and loved him, then according to Jesus, it is the Samaritan who loves God. Conversely, turning away from others, particularly those in desperate situations, is the same as turning away from God. Through this simple parable, Jesus teaches the priority of love over legalism and practice over dogma.

This parable told by Jesus reveals the core requirement and value for authentic discipleship. Espousing this value is not enough. Followers of Jesus must put this value into practice. The retreat ministry described in this book provides one example of such a practice. The positive impact on the lives of those who participated illustrates the value of a retreat ministry with transgender and gender non-conforming persons for faith communities. One participant expressed this impact in response to the question of whether the retreat affected current spiritual practices saying, "Yes. Renewed commitment to try opened doors to new writings!" Offering such a ministry of radical hospitality and spiritual companionship may serve as a beginning point for building new relationships of solidarity and agency with a much-marginalized population, especially if this is more than a single event.

The place to begin is connecting with local transgender and gender non-conforming people. Local advocacy groups or inclusive faith communities may be helpful. Participants in the retreat were very clear that transgender or gender non-conforming leadership is essential. I quickly discovered how important this was for some when I raised the question of an activity that would be led by a cis-gender person outside our group. Initially a congregation may function more in the role of a sponsor and support system than creating and leading the program and other aspects of the retreat.[20]

The three most basic elements necessary for a successful retreat are authentic hospitality and companionship; a safe space that includes basic essentials like good food, comfortable sleeping, green space, ease of access; and financial resources. Some faith communities are already in position to offer all three. For these communities, the next step is connecting with local transgender people and resources, and engaging the congregation in gender identity education if it is a new topic.

Other communities may not have a safe space to offer, but could provide financial support for hosting a retreat in another area, such as a retreat center, camp, building space of another congregation. Ease of access, accessibility of the buildings and rooms, and public transportation are important to consider. Confidentiality is another issue to keep in mind when planning space. Some places may be too public, too close to home, or not in a neighborhood known to be safe for gender non-conforming persons.

Financial support is also critical. For all of the reasons already stated many transgender people cannot afford the cost of a retreat. Fundraising or underwriting a retreat ministry in the budget are two possible methods to support this type of retreat ministry. Connecting with other faith communities or local and national advocacy agencies are additional avenues that may lead to financial support. Every location includes unique opportunities for creative fundraising. Funding the retreat so others can attend makes more than a practical difference. It is itself an act of radical hospitality that will be felt by those who receive.

The retreat is over. The information is analyzed and presented here. Every written and spoken reflection confirms that a retreat ministry may contribute to spiritual renewal and healing among people who identify as transgender or gender non-conforming. Jesus' story of The Good Samaritan points to and confirms the value and importance of such ministry in the context of being a good neighbor. The parable is not only for the benefit of the apparent victim left by the roadside. The act of the Samaritan initiates a process that affects at least three persons, including himself. Each person is changed through this act of mercy as new relationships are established.

20. A good beginning place is contacting PFLAGG, the Human Rights Campaign, or The National Center for Transgender Education. All of these organizations offer gender-identity study materials. My book, *In from the Wilderness*, also includes a study guide for congregations.

Like other stories of leaven and salt,[21] this parable reminds us that the transformation of a culture begins with small, almost invisible acts of faithful practice.

One overnight retreat dedicated to providing radical hospitality, spiritual companionship, and creative programming focused on spiritual renewal through the sharing of stories led several participants to reconsider the place of spiritual practices in their lives. Many spoke or wrote affirmatively about the importance of spiritual practices, and they expressed a desire to open the door to future possibilities and opportunities to participate in a safe faith community. The retreat functioned as spiritual leaven, expanding future possibilities and nourishing the retreatants. This was evident in the evaluations and interviews of those who participated in the creation, experience, and valuation of the retreat. This project convinced me of the importance and potential of such a ministry, and I hope to continue working with others who identify as transgender or gender non-conforming to create future retreat opportunities for our community and for those who host us. I hope it may encourage readers to consider a similar ministry. Imagine what lives may be transformed.

21. See Matthew 13:33; Luke 13:20–21; Matthew 5:13–16.

Appendix A

Prayer Weaving Tutorial[1]

Membering, Dismembering, & Re-Membering Reflection Through Paper Weaving

To Begin You Need:

- a hard copy of your 4-line prayer or story selection.
- 1 white or black square of paper (to place under your work and prevent ink/paint from getting on the table)
- 2 sheets of painted art paper (your directions will indicate when to get the paper)
- permanent markers or paint pens

You are invited to hold silence throughout the meditation.

If you have a question during the meditation, please ask Holly.

The Process: Membering

Reflection: Begin by reading your words slowly and silently, rereading them again and again.

What was it like to write your own words on the page? What form did it take?

---

1. Holly Benzenhafer, "Prayer Weaving Tutorial" created by The Rev. Holly Benzenhafer. Copyright, 2015.

What words, phrases, or concepts stand out to you as you meditatively read it now?

What is the direction of your thought? its theme, focus, or purpose?

How does reading it feel to you now?

Is any of it difficult or hard to say?

Does it resonate as true and authentic for you?

What is revealed about you, your perspective, and your theology within these words?

Action: Choose two (2) pieces of painted art paper and markers/paint pens.

Reflection: Gaze upon the pens and the two pieces of art paper noting the colors and textures of both sides.

Why did you choose these colors and not others?

What significance or meaning do you assign to them in this process?

Do you prefer one side of the art paper to the other—a side to show and a side to hide—or both?

What do your preferences (or lack of preference) indicate to you?

What does it feel like to infer meaning upon choosing a color?

Consider how you grant meaning to seemingly small choices in daily life.

Action: Return to the words your wrote and consider how you will place them on the two art papers. Using markers or paint pens, write your these same words on the paper. Experiment with different sizes or styles of writing. Try writing the same words repeatedly or in different directions. Add images. Allow the expression of your this part of your story and/or prayer to flow from your hands without evaluating or critiquing your process. Remember you have two sides to the paper with which to work. (If you use paint pens, allow adequate time to dry before turning the piece over.) On the reverse side, try changing the writing style or the arrangement of the words.

As you write and rewrite, imagine the colors and shapes of the words are holding a deeper, wordless prayer.

Reflection: When you complete placing the story/prayer on the paper, gaze upon each side of your art paper allowing yourself time to absorb how your words now inhabit the color and space.

What words stand out to you now? Why these words?

Do any of the sides of paper particularly resonate with you or seem jarring or vulnerable?

How is your story/prayer changing? How is it remaining constant?

Do you find yourself wanting to change the words–or actually rewriting them? Allow yourself time to sit with each side of the paper and ponder what deeper, wordless prayer or response may be forming within you before moving on.

(Note: If you wish to take a photo of the art paper for later reflection, do so now. Please do not disturb those around you with flash photography.)

The Process: Dismembering

Action (Cutting): When you are ready, it is time to cut the paper into 1/4-inch strips called *weavers*. To do this, you will use a pasta cutter (fettuccine setting). Bring both pieces of art paper to the cutter *making sure all paint is dry before proceeding.*

Pay close attention to how you feel watching the words of your prayer be cut into pieces. Notice how this action changes the way you perceive your story/prayer.

Reflection: When you have finished cutting your weavers, they will look similar to this picture.

Reflect upon your story/prayer now.

How does it feel in your hands?

What word or phrase from your story/prayer now stands out to you? Can you even remember the story/prayer, or has it changed into something new?

83

How might this shredding represent an area of your life you have tended that has been irreparably altered?

What does the shredding represent for you?

The Process: Re-Membering

Preparing the Weavers: Before working with each weaver, you will need to "civilize" it. Holding the weaver in one hand, use your other thumb to press the weaver against the edge of the table (not too hard). Then, pull the weaver between your thumb and the table. Turn it over, and repeat the process.

Civilizing the weaver softens it and makes it a little more pliable.

Action (Weaving): Begin to weave using the over-under plain weave technique. Weave in one weaver at a time on the right, vertical side.

Then, turn the whole piece a quarter-turn, clock-wise (to the right). After each turn, add a weaver.

Reflectively Play with the Weaving: Do you want a very balanced, even weave such at the one pictured, or are you going to try something unbalanced, perhaps cutting some of the weavers shorter or changing the colors frequently? If you know weaving techniques, you may want to try a different pattern.

Reflection: As you weave, consider how the colors blend. If your piece is stable enough, turn it over and look at the other side.

Which side speaks to you more?

Consider also your original story/prayer. It offers the accents of color to your piece, and it is no longer recognizable in its initial form.

Your story/prayer has also been dismembered and re-membered by your own hand. What has been gained and lost in this process?

Consider what it means to you—what is at stake—to have your words, your story, your prayer, altered . . . changed . . . destroyed . . . transformed . . . present . . . in this new form. Do you still claim it as your own?

What are other times in your life when membering, dismembering, and re-membering occur?

How might they be expressed?

Sharing: When your weaving reflection comes to an end, you may choose to leave your re-membered story/prayer for others to view at the end of our time. *Consider if you wish to also leave your original story/prayer for others to read while gazing and reflecting upon your weaving.*

If you choose to not have your story/prayer or weaving viewed, you can cover it with the square of paper used as your base during viewing.

Finishing: If you choose to make your weaving more permanent, use mounting tape (used in scrapbooking and to mount pictures) on one side of the weaving and affix it to a piece of heavy paper such as card stock. If you wish, you might add a copy of your original story/prayer, too. Or, you may find the story/prayer has taken a different language, form, and meaning from its initial writing via the weaving meditation process.

Appendix B

Participant Survey

Thank you for participating in this preliminary survey of the project. The following questions are designed to help us better understand your life experience, including participation in a faith-community, if sharing your transgender or gender-queer identity impacted your participation in this community, and how you describe your current spiritual path. Please leave blank any questions you prefer not to answer.

This is an anonymous form.

Please take as much time as you need to complete the following survey. When you have completed this form please email it to:_____

Part I: Personal history

1. Were you raised in a faith community? If so, how would you describe it?

2. How would you evaluate your experience in this community?

3. To what degree did this community meet your spiritual needs? Why or why not?

4. Did sharing your story as transgender/gender-queer impact your relationship with this community or others involved in it? Please describe:

5. Is this same faith community your present community? Why or why not?

Please use this space to share anything else about your faith community:

Part II: Personal spiritual journey

1. Do you think being transgender/gender-queer affects your spirituality? Why or why not? If so, in what way(s):

2. Has this gender identity influenced your current spiritual practices in any way? If so, how?

3. Has your spiritual community, direction, and/or path changed in any way because of acknowledging your gender identity? Please describe:

Part III: Your Space

This is space provided for you to share anything else about your spiritual life, practices, or anything else you would like to add.

Appendix C

Evaluation Form

Evaluation: "Narrative, Story, and Spiritual Autobiography as Positive Spiritual Practices: Spirituality in a Transgender/Gender-queer Context"

Thank you for participating in the retreat portion of this project. The following questions are designed to help me better understand your experience, evaluate the design, structure, and process of the retreat, and plan future retreat models specifically for and with transgender/gender-queer persons.

This is an anonymous form.

Please take as much time as you need to complete the following survey. When you have finished place it in the envelope provided and give it to the Project Director. Thank you!

Part I: Program

1. Did this experience meet your expectations? If so, in what way(s); if not, why not:

2. How would you evaluate the leadership/facilitation of the retreat?

3. To what degree did the retreat meet your spiritual needs? Why or why not?

4. What was the most helpful or inspiring part of this event? Please describe:

5. What would you want to add? Leave out?

6. Based upon this experience would you consider participating in a similar retreat? If so, what topic(s) or theme is of interest:

Please use this space to share anything else about program, leadership, or other content:

Part II: Technical/logistics

1. Please comment on the site location in terms of suitability for your needs?

   Timeframe?

   Aesthetics?

   Hospitality?

   Other?

2. Please comment on the food and accommodations: is there anything you would change?

Part III: Personal post-retreat spiritual evaluation

1. Do you think being transgender/gender-queer affects your spirituality? Why or why not? If so, in what way:

2. Has this retreat impacted your current spiritual practices in any way? If so, how?

3. Has your spiritual community, direction, and/or path changed in any way as a result of participating in this retreat? Please describe:

Part IV: Your Space

This is space provided for you to share anything else about your experience.

Appendix D

Follow-Up Interview Questions

1. Reflecting on your experience, what practices(s) or activities were most beneficial to you during the retreat?

2. Were there activities or practices that you found difficult or problematic in any way?

3. Was attending a retreat in which all the participants identified as transgender or gender-fluid beneficial for you? Why, or why not?

4. Would you be inclined to attend another, or recommend this type of retreat?

5. Is there anything else you would like to add?

Thank you for participating in this interview!

Appendix E

Annotated Sources
Participatory Action Research

Cameron, Helen, Deborah Bhatti, Catherine Duce, James Sweeney, Clare Watkins. *Talking About God in Practice: Theological Action Research and Practical Theology.* London: SCM, 2010.

> Combining Participatory Action Research with Theological reflection and practices the authors present a new model for engaging individuals and faith-based communities in transformational change. The text provides examples and practical guides for engaging in such a process.

Graham, Elaine. "Is Practical Theology a form of Action Research?" *International Journal of Practical Theology* 17 no. 1 (2013).

> In this article the author explores and compares the discipline of Practical Theology with Action Research. It is an especially helpful resource for persons engaged in any form of Action Research within faith communities or faith-based organizations.

Strand, Kerry, Sam Marullo, Nick Cutforth, Randy Stoecker, and Patrick Donohue. *Community-Based Research and Higher Education: Principles and Practices.* San Francisco: Jossey-Bass, 2003.

> The authors examine the principles and process of Participatory Action Research in relation to working with community-based organizations. It contains many useful examples and offers an interesting perspective of Particpatory Action Research in a secular setting.

Spirituality

Ammerman, Nancy Tatom. *Sacred Stories, Spiritual Tribes: Finding Religion in Everyday Life*. New York: Oxford University Press, 2014. Kindle.

The author examines the presence of religious and spiritual meaning in and through the ordinary events of daily life as shared through interviews with several Americans discussing what they value most in their lives.

Campolo, Tony and Michael Battle. *The Church Enslaved: A Spirituality of Racial Reconciliation*. Minneapolis, MN: Fortress, 2005.

This text on the historical relationship between racism and the Church in the United States offers insights and concepts helpful to thinking of the relationship between Transgender and genderqueer persons and the Church today.

Columba Stewart. "'We?' Reflections on Affinity and Dissonance in Reading Early Monastic Literature" *Spiritus*. Vol. 1. Baltimore: John's Hopkins University Press, 2001.

This article considers connecting points and barriers in understanding early Christian writings. The author raises issues such as cultural difference, context, and social and religious norms as obstacles to understanding.

Donohue-White, Patricia, "Reading Divine Maternity in Julian of Norwich." *Spiritus*. Vol. 5. Baltimore: John's Hopkins University Press, 2005.

Donohue-White reflects on the imagery of motherhood in Julian, noting positive aspects of the feminine in this imagery. She also raises concerns regarding conventional roles and interpretations of motherhood, noting the often unconscious concepts of motherhood the reader brings to the text.

Dreyer, Elizabeth A. and Mark S. Burrows. *Minding the Spirit: The Study of Christian Spirituality*. Baltimore: John's Hopkins University Press, 2005.

A collection of essays exploring the study of Christian spirituality from a variety of perspectives; as an academic discipline, the role of practice and interpretation, theological and historical, healing, and Aesthetics. This collection of essays by well-known scholars offers a wide-range of viewpoints, representing several disciplines.

Dupre, Louis and Don Saliers, eds. *Christian Spirituality: Post-Reformation and Modern.* New York: Crossroad, 1991.

> This collection of critical essays compares and contrasts Post-Reformation and modern forms of Christian Spirituality. It is a helpful resource for readers of Post-Reformation Christian spiritual texts.

Dyckman, Katherine, Mary Garvin, and Elizabeth Liebert. *The Spiritual Exercises Reclaimed: Uncovering Liberating Possibilities For Women.* Mahwah, NJ: Paulist, 2001.

> The authors present The Spiritual Exercises of Ignatius of Loyola within a framework of the particular experience and social situation faced by women. This analysis includes the need for women to balance self-care with caring for others, the impact of social factors such as sexism, economic insecurity, and single parenting on women and how such things affect spiritual development. Particular attention is given to the importance of listening to the "deep wisdom" of the self in the process of discernment.

Frankl, Viktor E. *Man's Search for Ultimate Meaning.* New York: Basic, 2000.

> Frankl explores the intersections of life and spirituality within the context of ultimate questions, the creation of meaning, and life as a spiritual quest.

Guigo II. *Ladder of Monks and Twelve Meditations.* Translated by Edmund Colledge and James Walsh. Collegeville, MN: Cistercian, 1979.

> This translation offers a helpful introduction what concisely explicates what the reader will discover in the actual texts while providing the historical context of Guigo II, including how little is actually known of his life. The Ladder of Monks describes Guigo II's vision of four rungs on a ladder as the four essential, ascending spiritual practices of reading scripture, meditation, prayer, and contemplation. The Ladder of Monks is considered a classic description of Lectio Divina.

Mollenkott, Virginia Ramey. *Sensuous Spirituality: Out from Fundamentalism.* Cleveland: Pilgrim, 2007.

> Dr. Mollenkott explores what she regards as misconceptions regarding human sexuality in teachings presented by the Church

and the power and possibility of the TLGBQ community to transform these misconceptions.

Spiritual Autobiography

Andrews, William L. *Sisters of the Spirit*. Bloomington, IN: Indiana University Press, 1986.

The author examines the autobiographical stories of three African-American Christian women living in Nineteenth Century America. The stories examine how each woman resolved her sense of vocational call with the racial, cultural and gender boundaries of that time.

Julian of Norwich: Showings. Translated by Edmund Colledge and James Walsh. Mahwah: N.J.: Paulist, 1978.

In this text Julian describes her theology as it developed through her dedication to The Church and personal spiritual experiences. One of the most dynamic aspects of Julian's theology is her theology of a gender-fluid Trinity. This is based upon her readings and visions. This includes gender-fluid language, such as God and Christ as Mother.

Kort, Wesley A. *Textual Intimacy: Autobiography and Religious Identity*. Charlottesville, VA: University of Virginia Press, 2012.

The author discusses the influences of defining oneself as religious in terms of autobiographical writing; and what such an identification may mean in terms of other descriptions of self-identity.

Leigh, David J. *Circuitous Journeys: Modern Spiritual Autobiography*. New York: Fordham University Press, 2000.

This text considers the complications of writing contemporary spiritual autobiography. The influences of culture, technology and contemporary ideas of the Self are among the topics discussed.

Mandelker, Amy, and Elizabeth Powers, eds. *Pilgrim Souls: A Collection of Spiritual Autobiographies*. New York: Simon & Schuster, 1990.

This is a broad collection of spiritual autobiographies from a variety of sources, genres and generations. It is an excellent resource for those interested in the construction and writing of spiritual autobiography.

Moore-Gilbert, Bart. *Postcolonial Life-Writing: Culture, Politics and Self-Representation*. New York: Routledge, 2009.

Moore-Gilbert provides an analysis of postcolonial and postmodern concepts of the Self and how relationality, embodiment, location, and continuity are affected in writing about the Self.

Morgan, Richard L. *Remembering Your Story: Creating Your Own Spiritual Autobiography*. Nashville: Upper Room, 2002.

In this text the author focuses on life as journey, drawing heavily upon chronological timeline in structure. He includes chapters considering writing spiritual autobiography from the perspective of connecting generations, facing life transitions, and healing memories. Morgan also stresses the unique value of every life; God speaks to humans through our stories; the Spirit works with us in our stories; it is possible to heal painful memories through stories; and stories create meaning throughout life.

Olney, James. *Memory and Narrative: The Weave of Life-Writing*. Chicago: University of Chicago Press, 1998.

In this text Olney presents a thorough exploration of the connections and problems regarding memory and the construction of personal narrative. Accuracy of recall over the passage of time, blending of memories, and other factors are discussed.

Peace, Richard. *Spiritual Autobiography: Discovering and Sharing Your Spiritual Story*. Colorado Springs: Navpress, 1998.

Written as a spiritual formation study guide for small groups, Peace's book offers a seven session structure that guides participants through theological, relational, and practical elements in writing spiritual stories. The book includes discussion of the content, process, preparation, and attentiveness involved in writing a spiritual autobiography.

Smith, Sidonie. *Reading Autobiography: A Guide for Interpreting Life Narratives.* 2nd ed. Minneapolis, MN: University of Minnesota Press, 2010.

While not specifically addressing spiritual autobiography, this is a good resource for teaching and working with groups on the topic of life writing, including spiritual autobiography.

Swan, Laura. *The Forgotten Desert Mothers: Sayings, Lives, and Stories of Early Christian Women.* New York: Paulist, 2001.

This collection of sayings and stories provides a glimpse into the spiritual lives and teachings of early Christian women and spiritual teachers, a voice often missing in the reading and study of Christian classics.

Weekley, David E. *In From the Wilderness: Sherman: She-r-man.* Eugene, OR: Wipf and Stock, 2011.

In this autobiographical text the author traces his life as a transgender person within the broader context of life as spiritual journey. This book presents a progressive theological view and interpretation of Scripture in relation to LGBTQ persons.

Phan, Peter C. and Jung Young Lee, eds. *Journey's at the Margin: Toward an Autobiographical Theology in Asian-American Perspective.* Collegeville, MN: Liturgical, 1999.

This book contains nine theological and autobiographical essays by Asian-American Theologians. Through the perspective of the marginality of Asian-Americans as a result of immigrant or refugee status and the experience of living on the margins of American culture, Phan connects this experience with other forms of marginality, hoping to create a more inclusive, equitable world. The editor's also discuss God's preferential love for the poor.

Spiritual Direction

Cameron, Julia. *The Artist's Way: A Spiritual Path to Higher Creativity*. New York: Penguin Putnam, 1992.

> The author offers a unique approach to creativity based upon writing and meditation as key spiritual practices. The exercises included provide tools for creative writing and journaling.

Guenther, Margaret. *Holy Listening: The Art of Spiritual Direction*. London: Cowley, 1992.

> Margaret Guenther discusses the critical importance of what she terms "Holy Listening" in the process of Spiritual Direction. The text also discusses how to prepare oneself for listening to others, and why such listening is an important spiritual practice.

Oden, Amy G. *God's Welcome: Hospitality for a Gospel-Hungry World*. Cleveland: Pilgrim, 2008.

> Oden discusses the spiritual practice of evangelism as hospitality and welcome in this book designed for study groups as well as individual use. The terms "hospitality" and "welcome" as defined and described are very broad and inclusive.

Painter, Christine Valters, and Betsey Beckman. *Awakening the Creative Spirit: Bringing the Arts to Spiritual Direction*. New York: Moorehouse Publishing, 2010.

> In this text the authors discuss the significance of the arts for Spiritual Direction and provide many tools and examples utilizing a variety of artistic media. Detailed examples and instructions are provided. This is an excellent resource for both individual and group use.

Paulsell, Stephanie. *Honoring the Body: Meditations on a Christian Practice*. San Francisco: Jossey-Bass, 2002.

> Paulsell examines embodiment, relationality, body and soul, and practices of positive expressions of embodiment. She considers examples such as bathing, clothing, and nourishing the body as a means of honoring the body.

Reiser, William. *Seeking God in All Things: Theology and Spiritual Direction*. Collegeville, MN: Liturgical, 2004.

In this text the author explores theological assumptions on topics such as prayer, revelation, and the Holy Spirit as these traditions function and influence Spiritual Direction.

Thompson, Marjorie J. *Soul Feast*. Louisville, KY: Westminster John Knox, 1995.

Following an introductory discussion concerning contemporary spiritual hunger the author presents and describes several practices for developing spiritual life. These include spiritual reading, prayer, fasting, confession, hospitality, and, ultimately, developing a Rule of Life for personal daily practice.

Tu-Tu, Desmond, and Mpho. *The Book of Forgiving: The Four-fold Path for Healing Ourselves and Our World*. New York: Harper One, 2014.

The authors present a method of forgiving that includes a valuable section on the significant role story telling plays in forgiveness and personal healing.

Vest, Norene, ed. *Tending the Holy: Spiritual Direction across Traditions*. New York: Moorehouse, 2003.

The essays contained within this text offer a wide variety of perspectives through which it is possible to develop an understanding of the unique benefits and challenges of engaging in spiritual direction from diverse traditions.

Wagner, Nick, ed. *Spiritual Direction in Context*. New York: Moorehouse, 2006.

This book presents several essays by various authors on the process of spiritual direction within specific contexts, including LGBTQ persons in the process of "coming out" to self, and, or others. Each author addresses the impact context may have on the process of spiritual direction.

Theology

Armstrong, Karen. *The Battle for God: A History of Fundamentalism*. New York: Random House, 2000.

> In this text the author traces the history of Jewish, Islam, and Christian fundamentalism as the result of social change rather than that of returning to earlier religious roots.

Cheng, Patrick S. *Radical Love: An Introduction to Queer Theology*. New York: Seabury, 2011.

> A text which considers the development of Queer Theology and challenges LGBTQ persons of faith to embrace and reflect God's "radical love." The author provides an overview of Queer theology, discussing how each person in the Trinity is an expression of divine, radical love, and what that means for LGBTQ persons of faith.

———. *From Sin to Amazing Grace: Discovering the Queer Christ*. New York: Seabury, 2012.

> Queer theologian Patrick Cheng considers traditional Christian doctrines of sin and grace through the lens of Queer Theology and what that implies for LGBTQ persons of faith.

Copeland, M. Shawn. *Enfleshing Freedom: Body, Race, and Being*. Minneapolis, MN: Fortress, 2010.

> This text explores the history of colonialism and its effects on minorities, particularly women of color, and the dynamics of current globalization as it seeks to reinforce traditional attitudes towards women, people of color, and sexual minorities within an anthropological theological framework.

Kraus, Donald. *Sex, Sacrifice, Shame, and Smiting: Is the Bible Always Right?* New York: Seabury, 2008.

> Krauss, Executive Editor for Bibles at Oxford University Press, explores whether areas exist in which the Bible is morally wrong, including topics such as vengeance, social marginalization, and the death penalty.

Miller-McLemore, Bonnie J., ed. *The Wiley-Blackwell Companion to Practical Theology.* Hoboken, NJ: John Wiley & Sons, 2011. Kindle.

This exhaustive volume examines how faith is shaped in everyday life. It explores our "meaning-making," suffering, and everyday acts of life as spiritual practices. From many perspectives and disciplines it examining the various methods employed in the study of practical theology within a global context.

Park, Andrew Sung. *From Hurt to Healing: A Theology of the Wounded.* Nashville: Abingdon, 2004.

Employing the religious Korean term "han" to define spiritual and psychic harm caused by unjust oppression, Park presents a model that moves toward healing and wholeness between the Church and those it has unjustly oppressed.

Sheldrake, Philip. *Spirituality and Theology: Christian Living and the Doctrine of God.* Mayknoll, NY: Darton Longman & Todd, 1999.

Chapter four of this text offers a reflection on Julian of Norwich and her theology of Trinity from the perspective of practice, maintaining that for Julian God is dynamic and active, performative and involved in the world and in human life. God's action in the world is revealed as, and through, love.

Soelle, Dorothee. *Suffering.* Philadelphia: Fortress, 1975. Kindle.

In this text Dorothee Soelle analyses traditional theologies of suffering and argues such theology is both unhealthy and an erroneous interpretation of the gospel. She then explores a positive theology of suffering as standing in solidarity with the marginalized and oppressed.

Taussig, Hal, ed. *A New New Testament: A Bible for the 21st Century Combining Traditional and Newly Discovered Texts.* New York: Houghton Mifflin Harcourt, 2013.

As indicated by the title this text provides both traditional and newly discovered texts including writings which include gender fluidity and variation from traditional gender roles.

Volf, Miroslav. *Exclusion and Embrace: A Theological Exploration of Identity, Otherness, and Reconciliation*. Nashville, TN: Abingdon, 1996.

> The appearance of being Other, of being different in some way, is often defined as itself evil. Miroslav Volf argues that if the healing word of the gospel is still to be heard today, Christian theology must find ways to address the hatred of the other.

Wolfteich, Claire E. "Practices of 'Unsaying': Michel de Certeau, Spirituality Studies, and Practical Theology" *Spiritus* 12. Baltimore: John Hopkins University Press, 2012.

> This article explores possible bridges between mysticism and practical theology. Employing Certeau as a dialogue partner the author proposes possible connecting points for conversation between spirituality studies and practical theology. The article suggests a continuation of the development of a "mystical-prophetic" practical theology grounded in the assertion that "practice precedes text; doctrine follows practice."

Transgender, Gender, and Sexuality

Bornstein, Kate. *My Gender Workbook: How to Become a Real Man, a Real Woman, the Real You or Something Else Entirely*. New York: Routledge, 1998.

> Kate Bornstein offers a thorough examination of gender, gender roles, and authenticity. Through conversation, humor and guided questions the author helps readers explore issues and questions about gender.

Butler, Judith. *Undoing Gender*. New York: Routledge, 2004.

> The author presents her theory that gender is a social construction for the purpose of regulating gender roles and human sexual expression.

Conover, Pat. *Transgender Good News*. Silver Springs, FL: New Wineskins, 2002.

> This text offers an overview of transgender experience from the perspective of a Transgender woman, including embodiment, social issues and a brief examination of selected Christian scriptures.

Annotated Sources

D'Emilio, John and Estelle B. Freedman. *Intimate Matters: A History of Sexuality in America*. New York, NY: Harper and Row, 1988.

> This text provides a detailed account of the history of tension between sexual liberty and cultural restraint, and social control over behavior.

DiNovo, Cheri. *Qu(e)erying Evangelism: Growing A Community From The Outside In*. Cleveland: Pilgrim, 2005.

> A narrative account of a pastor who explores ministry and theology as increasing numbers of transgender, gay, lesbian, bisexual and queer-identified persons begin visiting and attending her congregation.

Ehrensaft, Diane. *Gender born, gender made*. New York: The Experiment, 2011.

> This text specifically looks at gender-non-conforming children and includes personal stories from gender-non-conforming families.

Firer-Hinze, Christine and J. Patrick Hornbeck III. *More Than a Monologue: Sexual Diversity and the Catholic Church*. New York: Fordham University Press, 2014.

> This text is a collection of narratives expressing the diversity in sexual orientation and gender identity within the Catholic Church despite official teaching on these subjects.

Feinberg, Leslie. *Transgender Warriors: Making History from Joan of Arc To Dennis Rodman*. Boston: Beacon, 1996.

> A compendium of transgender history in which the author covers gender issues and behavior in several cultures, focusing primarily on the development of gender in western civilization.

———. *Transliberation: Beyond Pink or Blue*. Boston: Beacon, 1996.

> Feinberg provides compelling narrative and story to argue the need for celebrating human diversity in terms of gender identity and sexual orientation for the health and wholeness of all people.

———. *Stone Butch Blues*. Los Angeles: Aalysonbooks, 1993.

> In this novel Leslie Feinberg covers the landscape of transgender history through the eyes of a fictitious transgender character.

Foucault, Michel. *The History of Sexuality*. New York: Vintage, 1990.

> In this volume Foucault explores the employment of concepts and conversations around sex and sexuality as a means of social control and power.

Grant, Jamie M., Lisa Motett, Justin Tannis, et al. "Injustice at Every Turn: A Report of the National Transgender Discrimination Survey." National Center for Transgender Equality. Accessed February 16, 2016. http://www.transequality.org/.

> The results of a national survey of self-identified transgender persons conducted in 2006 illustrate the degree of discrimination and lack of resources facing this community.

Herdt, Gilbert, ed. *Third Sex, Third Gender: Beyond Sexual Dimorphism in Culture and History*. New York: Zone, 1994.

> A collection of essays refuting the binary concept of sexuality and gender.

Kinnaman, David, and Gabe Lyons. *Un-Christian: What a New Generation Really Thinks About Christianity . . . and Why it Matters*. Grand Rapids: Baker, 2007.

> Kinnaman and Lyons present solid research data based upon numerous interviews with young adults concerning why Christianity and the Church are irrelevant. Attitudes and actions towards transgender, lesbian, gay, bisexual, and queer-identified persons are named as primary reasons.

Kundtz, David J., and Bernard S. Schlager. *Ministry among God's Queer Folk*. Cleveland: Pilgrim, 2007.

> These authors offer practical tools as well as insights into the pastoral care of LGBT people. This is a helpful resource that provides an examination of some unique issues and counseling skills necessary for working with this population.

Annotated Sources

McCall-Tigert, Leanne, and Maren C. Tirabassi, eds. *Transgendering Faith: Identity, Sexuality and Spirituality*. Cleveland: Pilgrim, 2004.

> This collection of personal stories contains an overview of transgender persons in the Church. It also provides ideas for welcoming and creating inclusive liturgy and ritual for transgender persons of faith.

Martin, Dale B. *Sex and the Single Savior: Gender and Sexuality in Biblical Interpretation*. Louisville, KY: Westminster John Knox, 2006.

> This text explores and challenges common interpretations of gender and sexuality in biblical manuscripts.

Mollenkott, Virginia Ramey. *Omnigender: A Trans-Religious Approach*. Cleveland: Pilgrim, 2001.

> A dismantling of the traditional gender binary and examination of traditional Christian theology based upon the concept of a gender-continuum. The author offers a detailed examination of key Christian concepts such as the virgin birth from such a point of view.

Mollenkott, Virginia Ramey, and Vanessa Sheridan. *Transgender Journeys*. Cleveland: Pilgrim, 2003.

> This book explores the personal journey of two persons who come to identify as transgender and the many ways this impacts their lives and faith.

Prosser, Jay. *Second Skins*. New York: Columbia University Press, 1998.

> This text offers an in-depth analysis of transgender embodiment and lifts up the impact of deconstructionists who reject essentialism and affirm a gender binary as currently understood in popular western medicine.

Raushenbush, Paul Brandeis. "Christians Are a Cause of LGBT Oppression So We Have to Be a Part of the Liberation!" *The Huffington Post Online*. February 16, 2014. Accessed March 3, 2014.

> An excellent article discussing the role of the Church in creating the marginalization and oppression of LGBT people. Following

this overview the author argues that the church bears a responsibility to stand in solidarity with this same community in the process of liberation.

Rodriguez, E. M. "Did God Make Me This Way? Expanding Psychological Research on Queer Religiosity to Include Intersex and Transgender Individuals." *Psychology and Sexuality* 3, issue 3 (2012): 214–225.

This article examines how faith shapes the unique lives of intersex and transgender people. Though limited in scope the article does offer insights into the unique perspective and concerns of intersex and transgender individuals.

Sandstrom, Aleksandra. "Religious Groups Policies on Transgender Members Vary Widely." December 2, 2015. Accessed April 4, 2016. www.pewresearch.org/fact-tank/2015/12/02/religious-groups-policies-on-transgender-members-vary-widely/.

This research data provides a comprehensive examination of the attitudes and policies of various religious bodies towards those who identify as transgender and gender non-conforming.

Sheridan, Vanessa. *Crossing Over: Liberating the Transgender Christian.* Cleveland: Pilgrim, 2001.

In this work the author offers an analysis of Christianity that affirms the transgender experience.

Tanis, Justin. *Transgendered: Theology, Ministry, and Communities of Faith.* Cleveland: Pilgrim, 2003.

Tanis explores biblical texts pertaining to human gender and sexuality, reframing them from the perspective of current research and personal stories. This text present the concept of gender, particularly transgender, as a calling.

Tannahill, Reay. *Sex in History.* New York: Stein and Day, 1980.

In this volume Tannahill covers both known and less known aspects of norms and behaviors around sex and sexuality from prehistoric time to 1980.

Williams, Cristan. "Insidious: Extreme Pressures Faced by Transpeople." January 27, 2013. Accessed April 4, 2016. www.transadvocate.com/extreme-pressures-faced-by-trans-people n 8452.htm#sthash.usAY1be2.dpuf.

> The author explores daily life in the transgender community, lifting up the constant and unique stressors and pressures faced by this community.

Williams, Walter L. *The Spirit and the Flesh: Sexual Diversity in American Indian Culture.* Boston: Beacon, 1992.

> The author combines both a history of Native American sexual diversity and the impact of European colonization on sexual practices among these populations. The book includes a discussion of "Two-Spirit" and third gender concepts among many Native American communities and the impact of western colonization.

Addendum

A Suitable Methodology

Readings from Scripture, Christian mysticism, spiritual direction, practical theology, spiritual autobiography; and conversations with gender non-conforming and transgender persons impacted the search for an appropriate methodology for this project. Participatory Action Research emerged as an ideal model. During the process of research, writing, and creating a retreat, I revised the model through experience and reflection to resemble Theological Action Research (TAR) as described by Helen Cameron, Deborah Bhatti, Catherine Duce, James Sweeney and Clare Watkins in *Talking About God in Practice: Theological Action Research and Practical Theology*.[1] This chapter defines both participatory action research and theological action research and elucidates the process and reasons why the latter became the model for this project. The chapter may be especially helpful for faith-based communities or other groups considering providing a similar retreat experience for transgender persons.

Elizabeth Conde-Frazier describes the purpose of Practical Theology as recognizing and addressing the interplay between our being in the world and the purposes of God.[2] Such a theology is both contextual and transformational. It is contextual because it recognizes how theology is shaped by the historical, cultural, and other forms of community with which we

---

1. Helen Cameron et al, *Talking About God In Practice: Theological Action Research and Practical Theology* (London: SCM Press, 2010).

2. Bonnie J. Miller-McLemore,ed., *The Wiley Blackwell Companion to Practical Theology*, Vol. 63 (CITY, ST: John Wiley & Sons, 2011), 7377, Kindle.

identify.[3] It is transformational because this interplay is dynamic: our practices emerge from a particular context, and new understandings emerge as we engage life, which in turn affect our practices.

Conde-Frazier introduces the Spanish term "lo cotidiano" (the everyday) to highlight the central importance of paying attention to the everyday dynamics of people's lives:

> Lo cotidiano is a way of approaching theology as a space where God encounters those who are oppressed at the very place of their suffering. It allows one to see the impact of social sin and culture, class, race, gender, poverty, joblessness, and the daily routines and relationships of life on the religious and the political. People see the gaps between their theology and their lives and raise questions about God and ultimate meaning."[4]

Ideally, practical theology is not an abstraction removed from life, but rather one that names and addresses the injustices people and peoples face in life. In raising the question of possible tools for such an endeavor, Conde-Frazier names Participatory Action Research as a resource.

The connection Conde-Frazier draws between the methodology of Participatory Action Research and the task of naming and addressing injustices resonated with me and the others involved in this project. Creating and facilitating a retreat for gender non-conforming and transgender persons is not the same as creating and facilitating a retreat for other populations of people. This is a community that always brings histories of familial, social, and/or spiritual trauma and abuse in the form of rejection, ridicule, shame, bullying and, for many, ultimate isolation from former places of safety and comfort. This results in a high percentage of Post-Traumatic Stress Syndrome among transgender persons. For example, one article cited studies that indicate transgender people live under more extreme psychological pressures than even seen in active military personnel. While 55% of transgender persons live with social anxiety, similar types of anxiety are experienced by only 6.8% of the general population and by 8.2% of military personnel in the United States.[5] Failure to consider such history and statistics when planning a retreat for transgender people may result in a reduced

3. Ibid., 7370.

4. Ibid., 7390.

5. Cristan Williams, "Insidious: Extreme Pressures Faced by Trans People," *The Transadvocate*, January 29, 2013, accessed April 4, 2016, www.transadvocate.com/ extreme-pressures-faced-by-trans-people_n_8452.htm#sthash.usAY1be2.dpuf.

sense of safety and level of trust for participants. Instead, participants may experience increased anxiety, sense of risk, and loss of agency.

When retreat leaders understand and keep in mind statistics that describe the social reality of many transgender individuals, they can better create a safe and relaxing retreat experience. For example, knowing the prevalence of poverty among many transgender and gender non-conforming persons can inform important economic decisions, such as how to make the retreat available to everyone without cost.

Personal agency is another significant issue for many who identify as transgender. This includes having an acknowledged voice in events and gatherings focused on our community. In terms of this project it meant a model designed intentionally to give voice and build interaction among participants. While some methods objectify or diminish the role of participants either in a research study or retreat planning team, participatory action research as a method addresses the need for personal agency, egalitarian structure, and dynamic interaction, all of which are values expressed by transgender and gender non-conforming persons.

Participatory Action Research is community-based and defined by researcher Kerry Strand as composed of and influenced by three elements: 1. "popular education"-members of the community educating themselves in order to create social change; 2. "action research"-a means of improving the quality of life in a particular community through collaborative work between academicians/professionals and that community; and 3. "participatory research"-a process in which participants in the community are also included in the research project and process and its ultimate transformation during the progression from abstract theory to lived experience.[6]

In addition to other forms of research gleaned through the social sciences, this method of research includes practices such as narrative inquiry, interviews, and written and/or oral histories. As Conde-Frazier notes, oral histories and sharing stories are significant and powerful tools for creating agency among persons suffering from oppression. The open-ended use of questions and the use of sharing story often expands the horizon of experience, allowing for the creation of fresh insights and approaches to life.[7] These methodologies can be positive and powerful tools for a small group of transgender persons exploring spiritual autobiography and story

6. Miller-McLemore, 7411.

7. Miller-McLemore, 7480.

as sources of spiritual renewal; reclaiming and renaming the past to forge a healthier future.

These characteristics of participatory action research make it well suited for work with an oppressed community such as gender non-conforming and transgender persons. From the perspective of pastoral care and spiritual direction, however, a foundational dimension is missing. Theological Action Research (TAR) a branch of participatory action research addresses and adds this dimension. This particular type of participatory action research closely matches the characteristics of "holy listening,"[8] which includes the creation of a safe space for the purposes of spiritual refreshment and renewal:

> Spiritually, too, we cannot make it through the desert or across the frontier alone, but must depend on the kindness of strangers. Yet those strangers upon whom we depend are not really strangers, but our sisters and brothers in Christ. They are the hosts, the givers of hospitality, who sustain us along the journey, our spiritual friends and directors."[9]

A key component of such a space is attentiveness in presence and listening.[10]

The participatory structure and egalitarian process of Theological Action Research help create the kind of hospitable environment where holy listening can take place.

Authors Helen Cameron, Deborah Bhatti, Catherine Duce, James Sweeney and Clare Watkins offer this definition of Theological Action Research: "Theological Action Research is a partnership between an insider and an outsider team to undertake research and conversations answering theological questions about faithful practice in order to renew both theology and practice in the service of God's mission."[11] The key components of this definition: partnership, process, and theological conversation were important characteristics of this retreat project, and require further elaboration.

The first characteristic, partnership, is achieved in TAR by the formation of two "teams" that work collaboratively on the project. The terms "insider team" and "outsider team" are commonly used to designate each

8. See Guenther, "Holy Listening" chapter 1, "Welcoming the Stranger."

9. Ibid., 10.

10. Ibid., 1.

11. Cameron et al, 63.

group. The insider team is defined as those who "own" the practice that is the subject of the research. This group is dedicated to exploring and reflecting on the practice. The "outsider team" are those who facilitate the research and create opportunities for the insider team to participate in the research. The outsider team also brings a different perspective and knowledge to help expand and deepen theological reflection. The major reason for forming this insider-outsider relationship is to facilitate a variety of perspectives that stimulate reflection.[12] In this project I named myself, and others who assisted the project as the outsider team. The retreat participants composed the insider team. This dynamic relationship and variety of perspectives was further enhanced by the diversity of life experiences, gender identities, age, religious backgrounds, and spiritual practices represented by participants in the retreat.

Like other forms of Participatory Action Research, Theological Action Research employs data collection as part of the research process. An initial survey or questionnaire is completed by the inside team that gathers factual information and also invites and involves participants in the process of reflection.[13] An initial meeting or questionnaire completed by the inside team initiates the process. Additional information and a second invitation for feedback is provided through a written consent form that generally covers these issues:

- Confidentiality
- How data will be used
- Permission to record or film if applicable
- The voluntary nature of the study and assurance that participants can withdraw at any time
- There has been sufficient opportunity to read and understand information about the study, and to ask questions.[14]

I also included the option to receive a copy of the signed consent form, and extended the invitation to ask any questions about the research aspect of the retreat that might arise during our time together. I believe this increased the level of trust and agency, especially as we initially gathered at the retreat house.

12. Cameron et al, 64–65.
13. Cameron et al, 85.
14. Ibid., 94.

A final piece of the process is flexibility. As the authors of *Talking About God In Practice* note, unexpected things can happen that produce significant insights into the practice being studied.[15] For example, I had not met the new staff at the retreat center prior to our event. Based on earlier experiences with the one staff member I knew from other events I believed our group would be welcome. Still, as the one responsible for a safe environment I admit to having some anxiety. My concerns were unfounded. As we gathered and met staff, and throughout the retreat, the entire staff modeled exceptional hospitality, a welcome that embodied what Amy Oden describes as "gospel hospitality." Oden designates gospel hospitality in terms of being, not words. This means avoiding talking about the welcome God offers, and becoming the welcome God offers.[16] Each person present on the staff of our retreat center offered genuine gospel hospitality. This added to the quality of experience among all of us, and several retreatants made new friends among members of the staff.

Theological reflection and conversation evolve throughout the research project, but in terms of qualitative data, follow-up reflections by the insider team and outsider team are primary catalysts for conversation and future change.[17] Written data such as evaluation forms and follow-up interviews may be included as part of this process. In situations where Theological Action Research is engaged with faith-based organizations or parishes, it is at this point a conversation might emerge concerning future sessions of TAR.[18]

This project closely followed the TAR research process with a few modifications. One difference is that the research was engaged with a sample representing a particular community rather than an organization. Generally TAR is initiated by a specific religious body or faith-based organization that is seeking to solve or address some problem affecting the organization. This religious body then collaborates with a team that might include academicians, trained theologians, or other professionals. Together they work on creating a transformational solution to the specific issue. Given the modification of this project, the transgender and gender nonconforming retreat participants composed the insider group; the research

15. Cameron et al, 95.
16. Ibid., 113.
17. Ibid., 102–107.
18. Cameron et al,107.

team, which consisted of those who assisted me and myself, made up the outsider group.

A second variation from the traditional TAR model is that the groups did not meet face-to-face prior to the actual event. Each participant completed a questionnaire that asked about early religious history and experience, participation in a faith community, and personal spiritual journey.[19] These initial responses from the participants on the insider team became the first point of dynamic interaction in beginning to build a retreat specifically for transgender and gender non-conforming persons on the topic of story and spiritual autobiography as positive spiritual practices.

Reflection on this initial round of interaction led the outsider team to initiate a follow-up email asking participants for specific suggestions regarding the actual structure and content of the retreat. Participants were also asked if they had any practice they may like to lead during our time together, or if there were specific things they especially hoped to come away with following the retreat. As Helen Cameron et al. note, the presence of formal theologians and theologically trained facilitators may be very beneficial in TAR, but only so long as these persons are seen as participants and conversational companions.[20] One goal of this second round of conversations was to help establish an egalitarian atmosphere and respectful sense of agency among the participants. Providing an opportunity for input and leadership helped create this environment, and the suggestions and resources offered by some made significant differences in the final shape and schedule of the retreat.

One example of how responses from this second round of dialogue affected the structure of the retreat came through an insight gleaned through these conversations: I recognized that my concept of a retreat had been shaped by the classes, readings, and personal experience of recent years. This had led to a subconscious image of a retreat as somber, quiet, and filled with extended periods of time for personal reflection, writing, and rest. Email responses however indicated these participants envisioned a much different retreat.[21]

The initial questionnaire indicated that rather than a desire for prolonged periods of alone time there was a great amount of interest in

19. See Appendix I.

20. Cameron et al, 75.

21. Because of the interactive process of TAR, the final content and structure of a similar retreat may be very different.

opportunities for conversation and personal sharing. Three participants responded in the questionnaire that this was their first connection with a group of other transgender/ gender non-conforming people in any type of spiritually focused gathering. All of the participants expressed a hope to meet new friends and colleagues and make connections lasting longer than the retreat itself. Keeping these preferences in mind resulted in a retreat based on the need for more time together, more activities, and lots of opportunities for conversation, both in formal activities and unstructured time for informal small groups and conversation.

Another preference that emerged through TAR was for a design that included a variety of art forms and the sharing of personal story through social media art forms such as u-tube music and short videos. For example, prior to the retreat participants were invited to select a song that represented themselves and their lives in some way. A play-list was created and shared as one part of our time together. Only the person facilitating this activity knew which song belonged to whom. It was fun, enlightening and often moving to learn which person identified with which song, and why.

The number one response to what people hoped to take away with them was lasting connections with other transgender/gender non-conforming persons interested in story and spirituality. This desire was expressed by persons who worked full-time in transgender or lgbtq advocacy organizations and knew literally hundreds of gender non-conforming persons, as well as those for whom this retreat was the first time connecting with anyone else in the community.

This second conversation was followed by a third email letter in which participants were invited once again to offer suggestions in terms of structure or content for the retreat. This internet conversation took place shortly before the event and included several logistical questions ranging from special dietary or ambulatory needs to sleeping arrangements. The latter was important because the retreat house in which we were staying housed only fifteen persons, which was the exact number of our group. A mix of gender identities and special sleeping needs for two members of our group requiring CPAP (Continuous Positive Airway Pressure) machines, combined with a variety of room configurations made it challenging to create a housing chart. This limited space was further complicated in that some the rooms involved sharing a bathroom with an adjacent room. Aware that such conditions can be challenging for many people, and knowing that privacy is a core issue for many members of the transgender community

I included this concern in the email and sought the advice of other re-treatants. The group was able to solve these issues, first by checking and then acknowledging no one expressed a preference regarding a roommate or minded sharing a restroom, and secondly, by leaving options open once people arrived. For example, there were cots and extra bedding available in case someone desired a different type of sleeping space.

The questionnaire, email conversations and consent form created the kind of dynamic interplay between the insider group and outsider group described in Theological Action Research and together provided the input that ultimately resulted in the retreat described in this project. The additional pieces of data gathered were an evaluation form filled out by each participant at the end of the retreat, and the invitation to complete a written or oral post-retreat interview. These final pieces of data were valuable in evaluating this project, and will be invaluable in creating future retreat opportunities for persons who identify as transgender or gender non-conforming.

Engaging with the right method for this particular study and population resulted in the creation of a retreat which each participant helped create. No matter the degree of input given, virtually everyone expressed appreciation for the invitation to have a voice in the process. This creative dynamic, grounded in practical information and data about the unique challenges transgender persons face, combined with the dynamic, interactive tools designed through Theological Action Research propelled the momentum forward toward August and the time of actual gathering. As we assembled over the course of Friday evening and Saturday morning most people were meeting one another in person for the first time.

Bibliography

Andrews, William L. *Sisters of the Spirit*. Bloomington, IN: Indiana University Press, 1986.

Cameron, Helen, Deborah Bhatti, Catherin Duce, James Sweeney, and Clare Watkins. *Talking About God in Practice: Theological Action Research and Practical Theology*. London: SCM, 2010.

Cheng, Patrick. *Radical Love: An Introduction to Queer Theology*. New York: Seabury, 2011.

Conde-Frazier, Elizabeth. "Participatory Action Research." *The Wiley-Blackwell Companion to Practical Theology*. Edited by Bonnie J. Miller McLemore. New York: Wiley-Blackwell, 2012.

———. "Participatory Action Research: Practical Theology for Social Justice," *Religious Education* 101, no. 3 (Summer 2006): 321–329.

Feinberg, Leslie. *Transgender Warriors: Making History From Joan Of Arc To Dennis Rodman*. Boston: Beacon, 1996.

Fischer, Kathleen. *Women at the Well: Feminist Perspectives on Spiritual Direction*. New York: Paulist, 1991.

Frankl, Viktor E. *Man's Search for Ultimate Meaning*. New York: Basic, 2000.

GLAAD. http://www.glaad.org/publications/tdorkit.

Graham, Elaine. "Is Practical Theology a Form of 'Action Research'?" *International Journal of Practical Theology* 17 no. 1 (2013) 148–178.

Grant, Jamie M., Lisa A. Motett, Justin Tanis, Jack Harrison, Jody L. Herman, and Mara Keisling. "Injustice at Every Turn: A Report of the National Transgender Discrimination Survey," 2011. April 2013. http://www.thetaskforce.org/static_html/downloads/reports/reports/ntds_full.pdf.

Gray, Kathleen. "Exclusion of Transgender People Threatens Rights Bill." www.freep.com/story/news/local/michigan/2014/11/12.

Guenther, Margaret. *Holy Listening: The Art of Spiritual Direction*. Lanham, MD: Rowman and Littlefield, 1992.

Julian of Norwich. *Showings*. Translated by Edmund Colledge and James Walsh. New York: Paulist, 1978.

Jorgensen, Christine. *Christine Jorgensen: A Personal Autobiography*. San Francisco: Cleis, 2000.

Kowalewski, Brenda Marstellar. "Service-Learning Taken to a New Level through Community-Based Research," in *New Perspectives in Service Learning: Research to*

Advance the Field. Edited by Marshall Welch and Shelley H. Billig. Charlotte, NC: Information Age, 2004.

Mandelker, Amy and Elizabeth Powers, eds. *Pilgrim Souls: A Collection of Spiritual Autobiographies.* New York: Simon and Schuster, 1999.

Mikkola, Mari. "Feminist Perspectives on Sex and Gender." *Stanford Encyclopedia of Philsophy.* Updated January 29, 2016. http://plato.stanford.edu/entries/feminism-gender/#SexDis.

Moore-Gilbert, Bart. *Postcolonial Life-Writing: Culture, Politics, and Self-Representation.* New York: Routledge, 2009.

Oden, Amy G. *God's Welcome: Hospitality for a Gospel-Hungry World.* Cleveland: Pilgrim, 2008.

Peace, Richard. *Spiritual Autobiography.* Colorado Springs: Navpress, 1998.

Phan, Peter C. and Jung Young Lee, eds. *Journeys at the Margins: Toward an Autobiographical Theology in Asian-American Perspective.* Collegeville, MN: Liturgical, 1999.

Raushenbush, Paul Brandeis. "Christians Are a Cause of LGBT Oppression So We Have to Be a Part of the Liberation!" February 16, 2014. http://www.huffingtonpost.com/religion.

Sandstrom, Aleksandra. "Religious Groups Policies on Transgender Members Vary Widely." December 2, 2015. http://www.pewresearch.org/fact-tank/2015/12/02/religious-groups-policies-on-transgender-members-vary-widely/.

Strand, Kerry, Sam Marullo, Nick Cutforth, Randy Stoecker, and Patrick Donohue. *Community-Based Research and Higher Education: Principles and Practices.* San Francisco: Jossey-Bass, 2003.

Swan, Laura. *The Forgotten Desert Mothers: Sayings, Lives, and Stories of Early Christian Women.* New York: Paulist, 2001.

Tanis, Justin. *Transgendered: Theology, Ministry, and Communities of Faith.* Cleveland: Pilgrim, 2003.

Taussig, Hal, ed. *A New New Testament.* New York: Houghton Mifflin Harcourt, 2013.

The Center for Transgender Quality. "2015 National Transgender Discrimination Survey." http http://www.transequality.org/:

Thompson, Marjorie J. *Soul Feast: An Invitation to the Christian Spiritual Life.* Louisville, KY: Westminster John Knox, 2005.

Thompson, Peg. "The Coming Out Process in Spiritual Direction." *Spiritual Direction in Context.* Edited by Nick Wagner. New York: Morehouse, 2006.

Thor, Laura. "Living in the Image of God: Transgender People in Spiritual Direction." *Presence: An International Journal of Spiritual Direction* (December 2013).

Valters-Paintner, Christine, and Betsey Beckman. *Awakening the Creative Spirit: Bringing the Arts to Spiritual Direction.* New York: Morehouse, 2010.

Williams, Cristan. "Insidious: Extreme Pressures Faced by Transgender People." January 27, 2013. www.transadvocate.com/extreme-pressures-faced-by-trans-people_n_8452.htm#sthash.usAY1be2.dpuf.